BREAK THE GENERATION CURSE

By Marilyn Hickey

Marilyn Hickey Ministries
P.O. Box 17340
Denver, CO 80217

BREAK THE GENERATION CURSE

Copyright ©1988 by Marilyn Hickey Ministries
P.O. Box 17340
Denver, Colorado 80217
All Rights Reserved

ISBN 1-56441-004-8

*Special thanks to Jeanne Halsey
for making this book "readable"!*

All scriptures are quoted from the *King James Version*
of the Bible.

Printed in the United States of America

TABLE OF CONTENTS

INTRODUCTION

Here are two sides of the same coin:

". . . I the LORD thy God am a jealous God, visiting the iniquity of the fathers upon the children unto the third and fourth generation . . . " (Exodus 20:5)

and:

"Know therefore that the LORD thy God, he is God, the faithful God, which keepeth covenant and mercy with them that love him and keep his commandments to a thousand generations" Deuteronomy 7:9).

One day I counseled with a young woman who was going to divorce her husband. I asked, "Was your mother divorced?"

She said, "Yes."

I asked, "How many times?"

She answered, "Three."

"How many children did she have?"

"Four."

"How many times have you been married?"

She answered, "This is my third marriage."

I asked, "How many children do you have?"

She answered, "Three."

"Do you love your little girls?"

"Oh yes, I love my little girls!"

I said, "Do you know that they're going to grow up, and they're going to marry and divorce three times, and they're going to break your heart because your mother is under a generation sexual curse. She's been into all kinds of junk. You're in the same thing; you're making the same decisions. And you watch—your little girls will too."

Her face looked as if I had slapped her, but we'd better get slapped with the Word so we don't make a big fat mistake. That same night I got a call, and she said she wasn't leaving her husband!

Do you want to be blessed? Do you want your children to be blessed? Nothing touches you more than your children. When you give place to God in your life, you open yourself to His blessing. But if you give place to the devil—or if you are under a "generation curse"—you are asking for your children to enter into the same curse, and the devil will devour them!

Listen to this true story of two American families:

Max Jukes was an atheist who married a godless woman. Some 560 descendants were traced:

Three hundred ten died as paupers—150 became criminals—seven of them murderers—100 were known to be drunkards—and more than half of the women were prostitutes.

The descendants of Max Jukes cost the United States government more than $1.25 million in 19th century dollars.

Jonathan Edwards was a contemporary of Max Jukes. He was a committed Christian who gave God first place in his life. He married a godly young lady, and some 1,394 descendants were traced:

Two hundred ninety-five graduated from college, of whom thirteen became college presidents and 65 became professors—three were elected as United States senators—three as state governors, and others were sent as ministers to foreign countries—30 were judges—100 were lawyers (one the dean of an outstanding law school)—56 practiced as physicians (one was the dean of a medical school)—75 became officers in the military—100 were well-known missionaries, preachers and prominent authors—another 80 held some form of public office, of whom three were mayors of large cities—one was the comptroller of the U.S. Treasury—and another was vice president of the United States. [1]

Not one of the descendants of the Edwards family was a liability to the government!

If you follow God—serving Him, praying, living in the Word, keeping committed to Him—then your children and your grand-children are going to grow up and give the devil a hard time:

> *Behold, I set before you this day a blessing and a curse; A blessing, if ye obey the commandments of the LORD your God, which I command you this day: And a curse, if ye will not obey the commandments of the LORD your God, . . .* (Deuteronomy 11:26-28).

> *And it shall come to pass, if thou shalt hearken diligently unto the voice of the LORD thy God, to observe and to do all his commandments which I command thee this day, that the LORD thy God will set thee on high above all nations of the earth: and all these blessings shall come on thee, and overtake thee, if thou shalt hearken unto the voice of the LORD thy God* (Deuteronomy 28:1,2).

Who knows how many senators or judges or presidents will come out of our families? People who serve God are going to produce godly seed!

1 Gibson, Noel and Phyl. EVICTING DEMONIC SQUATTERS & BREAKING BONDAGES. Drummoyne: Freedom In Christ Ministries Trust, 1987.

Chapter One

GETTING OUT FROM UNDER THE CURSE

AUTHOR'S NOTE: In a lengthy, well-documented letter written to Marilyn Hickey Ministries in the spring of 1988, Delvin and Annette L— of North Dakota shared a modern-day account of dealing with a curse on their land. Midwestern American farmers have suffered tremendously the past several years, but this young couple discovered how to overcome the evil works of the enemy! Read on . . .

> " . . . *they overcame him by the blood of the Lamb, and by the word of their testimony; . . . "* (Revelation 12:11).

Delvin and I were married nine years ago, and we moved onto his family farm where he was raised and had lived for the last 33 years. Delvin's parents had moved there in 1949, and his grandparents had also lived there. We signed the papers to purchase the family farmstead in 1979.

We both gave our hearts to the Lord in January of 1983, and as we began to let our light shine into a lost and dark world, so also began the devil's attempts to destroy our Christian testimony.

It soon became apparent that we were under "the curse." We saw attacks on our physical lives which were mostly

1

hereditary. I experienced a tubal pregnancy and a miscarriage, and had problems with allergies. Later, our children suffered birth defects, broken bones, and speech impediments.

Financially, our troubles arose in the fall of 1983. We realized our land payments had been deferred for three years, and now they would have to be paid. It made things look very bleak. We spoke to our Farm Home Administration (FHA) supervisor, who was a born-again believer (isn't God merciful!). We asked him what our financial outlook was, and it was as if the Holy Spirit spoke right through him to us: "Unless things change, you will only be able to hold onto the farm for another four years."

We had already experienced a severe drought in 1980. Then came several years of large numbers of grasshoppers, which destroyed much of the crops and their yield. At this time, cattle prices were low. Adding to the already-low prices, we had large cattle losses due to sickness.

We also were fighting a noxious weed called "leafy spurge," which had badly infected all of our pastures and rangeland. No animal could eat it, and we could hardly find anything that could kill it. We spent thousands of dollars on herbicides, trying to stop the leafy spurge from spreading, but we saw no improvements.

It was the end of October, 1985—the day before I delivered our third child—that the Lord quickened to me His words in Hosea 4:6:

> *My people are destroyed for lack of knowledge: because thou hast rejected knowledge, I will also reject thee, . . . seeing thou hast forgotten the law of thy God, I will also forget thy children.*

The next day our little girl was born with a birth defect, and then a deadly infection. One month later, on Thanksgiving Day, our born-again family doctor looked at our four-week-old baby and said, "We need divine help."

Little Brittany had gone through surgery twice that week; neither surgery had been successful. The infection was not detected immediately, and that stopped the natural healing process in her body, which weighed only 5 pounds. God's words in Hosea 4:6 ominously came back to me.

We prayed for "knowledge." With all the faith we had, we asked God to spare our little girl. Prayers had been going up from every source who knew of our situation . . . and God mercifully honored them.

The next morning the nurses informed me that Brittany had miraculously gained 9 ounces since they had last weighed her the previous morning (anyone who has ever had a small baby in the Intensive Care Unit will know how closely they watch the baby's weight, counting every quarter-ounce). God had intervened and shown us His mercy. We thanked Him and, as Brittany recovered, we brought her home.

Searching Out the Curse

But on that Thanksgiving Day, we knew we must press on. We needed to become more knowledgeable of God's Word, and we needed to understand His law. Our hearts were set on finding out what Hosea 4:6 really meant for us today.

We had heard so many arguments: "That's all Old Testament . . . We are not under the law anymore, we are now under grace . . . ." There was no doubt that we were under God's grace—and that He had indeed been gracious to us in sparing our little girl—but there *must* be more.

As we searched the Scriptures, God began to open the eyes of our understanding. He enlightened us (Ephesians 1:17-20) that we might be filled with the *knowledge* of His will, in all wisdom and spiritual *understanding* (Colossians 1:9-12).

I had continually read these scriptures to my little girl:

"Blessed shall be the fruit of thy body, . . . " (Deuteronomy 28.4).

"Christ hath redeemed us from the curse of the law, being made a curse for us: for it is written, Cursed is every one that hangeth on a tree" (Galatians 3:13).

But then we began to read all of Deuteronomy 28 very closely. Verse one says:

And it shall come to pass, if thou shalt hearken diligently unto the voice of the LORD thy God, to observe and to do all his commandments which I command thee this day, that the LORD thy God will set thee on high above all nations of the earth.

This is where we wanted to be.

Verses 2 and 3 said:

And all these blessings shall come on thee, and overtake thee, if thou shalt hearken unto the voice of the LORD thy God. Blessed shalt thou be in the city, and blessed shalt thou be in the field.

"In the field. . . ." That got our attention because, as farmers and ranchers, we knew God was talking about blessing **our fields.**

We read on:

And the LORD shall make thee plenteous in goods, in the fruit of thy body, and in the fruit of thy cattle, and in the fruit of thy ground, in the land which the LORD sware unto thy fathers to give thee (verse 11).

Oh, how this applied to us!

> *The LORD shall open unto thee his good treasure, the heaven to give the rain unto thy land in his season, and to bless all the work of thine hand: . . .* (verse 12).

We felt excitement building inside us, for here were all of God's promises that any farmer or rancher could ever ask for! We needed God's blessings upon the work of our hands, the promise of rain in due season, and His blessings upon our ground, our cattle, and our fields!

Now we read verse 15:

> *But it shall come to pass, if thou wilt not hearken unto the voice of the LORD thy God, to observe to do all his commandments and his statutes which I command thee this day; that all these **curses** shall come upon thee, and overtake thee.*

As we read through the list of curses, we knew we were under "the curse" and were being overtaken by it!

We were carrying "*. . . much seed out into the field, and . . . gather(ed) but little in; for the locust . . . consume(d) it*" (verse 38); we had grasshoppers destroying crops, hay land, and pastures (verses 21 and 42); our crops failed because of drought (verse 24); our cattle were being killed by lightning and snowstorms, besides sickness, disease, and dying at birth (verses 31 and 51).

We were also fighting a no-win battle with the leafy spurge. Besides the time and money spent, we were also putting on the ground a chemical which does not break down with time. In our attempts to kill the leafy spurge, we applied this chemical which went through the soil in the same hazardous form as when it was applied, entering into our ground water, and being washed into our surface water. We were probably infecting numerous wildlife, and maybe even causing more harmful side effects than were known to us.

"Well, every farmer and rancher has some crop failures and cattle losses. It's part of being in the farming business." Yes, but when God's people have losses mounting up so high that you begin to perish off the land (Leviticus 18:25), something is wrong! We needed God's help desperately if we were to keep the family farm.

God Speaks . . . And We Listen

One night at our church service, there came a word of knowledge. The Lord spoke to us, "I **am** the God Who heals your little children." God was getting our attention, and His words were confirmation to us that He was caring for our little girl.

Next He said, "You are not to look to the government for help, but to look to Me to supply all your needs." In this age, with all our governmental programs—especially in the farm business—we knew He was again speaking to us. As we faced the financial problems, God promised us His blessings . . . and told us we would be successful!

The end of April 1986 found us in a wild snowstorm. The cows were nearly finished calving, which meant there was a baby running alongside of every cow, and we had already turned them out in the open range.

During the night of the snowstorm, we tried to get to them to help care for the baby calves, but it was impossible in the storm to see anything, and we were forced to turn back. When we were back in the house, we knew all we could do was pray.

We asked God to put His hand over the cattle and to protect every one of them, that not one would be lost. Peace filled our hearts, and we went to sleep knowing that all was well in God's hands.

Setback

The storm continued until late the next evening, and although it was nearly dark, we went out expecting to see a miracle. Instead, we found one . . . then two . . . and three dead calves. By the following morning, the number of dead calves came to seven! What had happened?

Didn't we have enough faith to believe? Wasn't God's hand protecting over us, His people? We knew that Romans 8:28 says, " . . . *all things work together for good to them that love God,* . . . " We loved the Lord, so we began to pray and read the Word more earnestly.

Soon God brought us into Leviticus 19:19:

> *"Ye shall keep my statutes. Thou shalt not let thy cattle gender with a diverse kind: thou shalt not sow thy field with mingled seed: . . . "*

This revelation brought us to the conclusion that God had—from the beginning—wanted man to know how important it was to maintain strict segregation of everything, even His cattle.

The marginal notes in our Bible said, "God wished everything preserved after his kind, so that the distinct colors, types, sizes, and kinds could continue according to His plan, forever."

God discouraged the crossbreeding of animals and the mixing of seed by commandment in accordance with His fixed and eternal law (Genesis 1:11,12,21,24,26-28; Deuteronomy 32:8; Acts 17:26). We knew this to be true for Israel because every time they mixed with the heathen nations around them, they fell into sin, ended up in discord, and suffered many consequences.

We were in direct disobedience to God's Word, for over the

years we had been crossbreeding our cattle with five or six different kinds. We began to see light as we read Leviticus 18:25:

> *"And the land is defiled: therefore I do visit the iniquity thereof upon it, and the land itself vomiteth out her inhabitants."*

This also agreed with what we read in Deuteronomy 28:45,46:

> *Moreover all these curses shall come upon thee, and shall pursue thee, and overtake thee, till thou be destroyed; because thou hearkenedst not unto the voice of the LORD thy God, to keep his command- ments and his statutes which he commanded thee: And they shall be upon thee for a sign and for a wonder, and upon thy seed for ever.*

By now we had experienced enough pain and suffering not to want to doubt God's Word! So we read the Word of God, and we did not doubt, but believed that *God's Word was true.* We accepted it without question, standing on John 17:17, *" . . . thy word is truth."* And the truth would set us free.

We knew that *His Word never changes because He never changes.* Jesus said in Matthew 24:35, *"Heaven and earth shall pass away, but my words shall not pass away."*

Now we saw that *keeping God's Word was the secret to His blessings.* We saw that God's Word—whether in the Old Testament or in the New Testament, whether "under law" or "under grace"—still has requirements which have to be met!

Perseverance

We understood that God's grace in the New Testament did not excuse us from sin or allow us to do the very things He had forbidden His people to do in the Old Testament. We saw that we could be children of God and, at the same time, have the "curse" working in our lives . . . and this gave us the answer to so many of our troubles!

The Lord directed my husband and me to alternately fast for a 21-day period, believing that we were facing what Jesus meant when He said, *"Howbeit this kind goeth not out but by prayer and fasting"* (Matthew 17:21).

Twice I felt like quitting the fast, and I told Delvin I was going to stop. But in those weak moments, God quickened His Word to me again:

> ... *Fear not, Daniel: for from the first day that thou didst* **set thine heart to understand, and to chasten thyself before thy God,** *thy words were heard; and I am come for thy words. But the prince of the kingdom of Persia withstood me one and twenty days: . . .* (Daniel 10:12,13).

I was encouraged as I let God's words minister to me.

While reading in Daniel, I also read chapter 9, where Daniel was confessing sin and praying to God to hear his supplications. I noticed that verse 11 spoke of *"the curse"* being poured upon us. We were beginning to understand God's Word.

On the twenty-first day of our fast, we had a breakthrough! Up to this time, we had not shared the details of our situation with anyone except Peggy, a sister in the Lord whom we had asked to pray concerning our finances. As she interceded for us, God told her **to deliver our land.**

At the exact time we broke our fast, Peggy was at her house, engaged in praise and worship. She did not know that we had fasted for 21 days, nor that the 21 days were ended. While worshiping, she was slain in the spirit, and God revealed His will about how our deliverance from the curse was to take place.

On April 6, 1987—we call it "D-Day"—Peggy started out on the usual road to our farm, but she was turned back because of road construction. She phoned to tell us she was still coming, but she needed new directions on how to get out here. We told her how to take another road, which she soon did.

While on this other road, the devil again tried to prevent her by throwing her car into the ditch. After bringing her car back onto the road, Peggy stopped to check that no one was hurt and nothing was damaged. God assured her of His angels which He had sent to surround her and our farm.

We knew how much the enemy did not want this land to be delivered from the curse. It meant Satan and all his demons would have to be gone in the name of Jesus. When Peggy arrived safely, Delvin and she went out onto the land, and they began to break the curses.

Here is Peggy's story:
Intercession

"I was praying diligently for Delvin and Annette and their situation on the ranch. Because I was unlearned in the ranching operation, I really didn't know how to pray specifically for them, so I sought God, asking how I could help them. The answer came quickly, 'Deliver their land.'

"The Lord had used me in deliverance before, but never for land. I believed it was scriptural—according to Ephesians 6:12 and Daniel 10:13—and I knew in time He would show me how and where the deliverance would come.

"God began to show me that He gives us the choice between curses and blessings (Deuteronomy 11:26-28, 27:15-26, 28:1-14). He showed me that Delvin and Annette's lack of prosperity and the problems dealing with their land were because God had been true to His Word: **He had cursed their land** due to past sins which had been committed there.

"Leviticus 18:25 shows us that land can be defiled, and God visits iniquity upon it. Iniquity in the Old Testament means rebellion, and evil consequences and judgments come upon rebellion.

"His Word states that a curse can be passed on down from generation to generation (Exodus 20:3-6). We are not guilty of our ancestors' sins, but we do suffer the consequences of their disobedience if those sins are not dealt with scripturally.

"The Lord gave me a word of knowledge dealing with past sins that had been committed on their land of which Delvin and Annette were unaware. They knew Native Americans had once settled, lived, and worshiped on their land (they live within a half-mile of a Sioux Indian Reservation). To this day, tepee rings can be found, along with other small artifacts, such as arrowheads.

"The ancient worship of Indian gods on their land was an example of Exodus 20:3-6. Iniquity was visited upon the land, and the result was leafy spurge. The reason man cannot seem to completely control and find a way to permanently kill this noxious weed is that it is one of God's ways of visiting iniquity upon the land.

"On the day of the deliverance, the Holy Spirit showed us how to break the curses. Past and present sins had to be confessed, and forgiveness was required. One must forgive the people who were the cause of the iniquity.

"One has to now choose to be obedient to God's law, and commit oneself to following it. Any abominable things dealing with witchcraft or with the worship of false gods which are in your possession must be destroyed (Deuteronomy 7:25,26).

"Of course, all of this must be done in complete faith in God's Word and in Jesus Christ. Believing that Christ became a curse for us—as stated in Galatians 3:13,14—we now can share in

11

the blessings of Abraham if we choose to walk in obedience to God's Word."

Deliverance!

After the spiritual battle was won, it was time to start doing something. We had not yet made out a farm plan for 1987 at our FHA office, knowing there would not be any operating money loaned to us this year because of the previous year's unpaid debt.

Our harvest in 1986 was destroyed by high winds and heavy rains. Ninety-five acres of wheat was harvested in the middle of October, but because of all the wet conditions, it was ruined and could not be sold. We gave it to a neighbor for pig feed in exchange for the use of his hay equipment. Out of 110 acres of corn, sixty acres were totally lost and had to be plowed under; the other fifty acres we managed to feed to our cattle.

On May 5 we walked into the loan office at the FHA, trusting God to work out **His plan** for our farm this year. FHA agreed to release money from the sale of twelve cull (the worst of the herd) cows and nine yearlings, which would be used for us to operate and live on.

We were able to purchase our seed and the needed fuel to get the crops in on time. We sold some of our crossbreed bulls and bought back purebred bulls in obedience to God's Word. The man we bought them from showed his kindness by letting us use another of his bulls *free.* We knew God was at work, helping us every step of the way.

We were again led to fast and pray for another 21 days. We did not know why, but we were obedient. When we got to the last three days of the 21-day fast, the Lord began to reveal something to us.

It was a beautiful Sunday morning on June 14, when Delvin

insisted I go along with him to check the cattle. As we came through one of the pastures, Delvin got out to open the gate. As he did, he noticed something. He said, "Ann! Look!" *The leafy spurge was dying everywhere.* We got out to take a closer look, and we could see the leaves were dead, and it was drying up from the bottom.

Delvin recalled that when he and Peggy prayed to break the curses off the land, they were led to reverse the curse on the leafy spurge, cursing it to its roots. We finished our cattle check and took a close look at all the leafy spurge, which was dying everywhere. When we got home, we offered up a sacrifice of thanksgiving, praising and worshiping Jesus for what **He** had done!

The next day Peggy came out with her camera and took pictures of the leafy spurge. In the middle of June, leafy spurge should be in its peak, blooming with bright yellow flowers. As we looked out across our land, the leafy spurge looked like it does in the fall: it was brown and drying up. Never had we seen anything like it.

We had not applied any chemical sprays or herbicides this spring, yet it looked like we had. It was so obvious that something was working against the spread of this noxious weed. God was truly performing a miracle before our eyes!

The Curse Is Reversed

As summer continued, the rains came in due season, but the leafy spurge continued to die out. Our work was done on time, and our harvest was ready. We had planted 100 acres of barley, which produced 40 bushels to the acre (our average yields were always low, ranging from 15 to 25 bushels per acre)! It was the best yield Delvin ever had.

Our grain bins were full, and we had to stockpile some on

the ground. Our 130 acres of corn produced abundantly, and we were able to harvest every acre!

Through the summer we noticed we were producing more with less money spent than ever before. Our repairs—which had always been large and very costly—were now almost none. My garden also turned out to be the best harvest I had ever raised. I was even able to take a week's vacation because of God's gracious provisions.

We began to reap the blessings of God's promises for the first time. We began to win lost souls for the Lord (until this time, we had never led anyone to salvation). There's a big difference in the way this family farm operation is run because Jesus is Lord, His Word is true, and He has set us free from the curse! Because of the knowledge we gained in taking God at His Word, we no longer have to be defeated Christians. Praise God!

Chapter Two
WHAT BRINGS THE CURSE

I was so blessed by Delvin and Annette's true-life testimony! When we received their letter at our office, they also sent several photographs of the "leafy spurge" plants dying, legal documents showing how much their farm indebtedness had been, and even advertisements showing man's (ineffective) attempts to correct their weed problem . . . when the *real* problem was an ancient curse upon their land!

Many of the health problems that Delvin and Annette and their children suffered were probably hereditary, but the curse on their land was not brought on by their own sin or even the sins of their forefathers . . . but by the previous inhabitants (the Sioux Indians) of their property! Until they broke the curse off their land, their very lives were at stake.

Most Christians really try to walk in the light of God's Word, and they often check on themselves to see if they're sinning against God in some way or another. Then you realize that you can come under a curse for which you are personally not responsible but have inherited, either through your ancestors or through someone else. That's bad news!

"But Marilyn, what are you talking about? What do ancient curses have to do with my life today?"

I'm glad you asked that! God has been dealing with me for a long time about blessings and curses. Awhile ago, I became concerned about some of the things that have gone on in the lives of people to whom we've ministered. Terrible things were happening—asthma, cancer, obesity, alcoholism, heart conditions—and God began to show me, piece by piece, where these awful things really came from.

These things that harass and plague us are actually *family or generation curses* . . . problems which started way back with our ancestors and have been carried through right to today. What's worse, they won't stop here, but can be passed on to our children and to our children's children!

The World Knows

Even the world is aware of this because when you fill out an insurance form of any kind, they always ask, "Is there a history of heart disease in your family?" or "Diabetes?" or "Cancer?" or "Mental illness?" Now why do they ask that? Because they believe that if such problems or diseases are in your background, you could have it too.

The mother of a woman on our staff died of an asthma-like condition. Sure enough, this woman began to suffer the same symptoms which had killed her mother. She began to have the same old junk and garbage start destroying her health. I believe that an evil spirit of disease had attacked the mother; and then when she died, he waited for the next generation to attack again. When weakness comes down, the enemy comes down and attacks too.

Wally and I have an adopted son, Michael. Mike was three and a half when we adopted him, and he has experienced all sorts of problems through the years. I used to wonder, "Well, we raised him right. We did this right, and we did that right. Why does he still experience such difficulties?"

Of course, we did some things wrong; there's no question that we did, and we repented of the things we did wrong. But I thought, "I never taught him to do these things, so where did that come from?"

Then I began to see that these hideous things come down

from generation to generation, attacking one family member after the next. Mike didn't get those problems from Wally or me; he got them from somewhere way back in his biological family's history. But we're his adopted and spiritual family, and we've taken authority over the problems and have released him from the curse!

Some Family History

I was visiting my 83-year-old aunt in Sewickley, Pennsylvania. She was so healthy and doing so well. I asked her, "What is the longevity of our family?"

My maiden name is Sweitzer, and she answered, "Well, the Sweitzers have a history of heart trouble. Most of them die of heart trouble." She began to tell me about their life spans.

She also told me about my maternal grandmother. "Those are the ones who have the real longevity; they do not have heart problems."

I had a heart problem, but I didn't realize that it had come from my father's background. I was healed of that heart condition because I claimed that Jesus Christ came to break the curse for me! So when I heard about my father's history of heart trouble, I began to break that curse over my daughter Sarah's life.

I know that Sarah is not going to have a heart problem. The devil is not going to come out and attack Sarah . . . and Sarah's children and grandchildren aren't going to have heart problems either because we've stopped the devil in his tracks! So a lot of the things we've encountered that attack our children are actually *family curses*, curses which are passed down from generation to generation.

Noah Got Drunk

Let's see what the Bible has to say about this. In Genesis 9, we see how this thing starts:

> *And Noah began to be an husbandman, and he planted a vineyard: And he drank of the wine, and was drunken; and he was uncovered within his tent. And Ham, the father of Canaan, saw the nakedness of his father, and told his two brethren without. And Shem and Japheth took a garment, and laid it upon both their shoulders, and went backward, and covered the nakedness of their father; and their faces were backward, and they saw not their father's nakedness. And Noah awoke from his wine, and knew what his younger son had done unto him. And he said, Cursed be Canaan; a servant of servants shall he be unto his brethren. And he said, Blessed be the LORD God of Shem; and Canaan shall be his servant. God shall enlarge Japheth, and he shall dwell in the tents of Shem; and Canaan shall be his servant* (Genesis 9:20-27).

Here is actually a picture of the beginning of a family curse. Proverbs 26:2 says, " . . . *the curse causeless shall not come.*" If we see sin and various things happen in our family, that sin is always a curse. Sickness is always a part of the curse. Poverty can pass from generation to generation. God's Word says, "It didn't just come on its own—there is a cause for it."

Now Noah got drunk. Alcohol is one of the devil's favorite tools to open the door to a hideous curse. You can talk about social drinking all day long, but I tell you: **alcoholism is not so much a sickness as it is a sin.** And sin brings a curse.

Another woman on our staff told me that her grandfather was an alcoholic; and her father was an alcoholic; and then her brother was an alcoholic. That's a curse, and it comes down through the generations.

Noah got drunk. When people get drunk they do things they wouldn't normally do because their will is broken down. What happened to Noah was that he was uncovered in the tent. *Uncovered* in Hebrew indicates there was a homosexual act.

Habakkuk 2:15,16 tells us about this:

> *Woe unto him that giveth his neighbour drink, that puttest thy bottle to him, and makest him drunken also, that thou mayest look on their nakedness! Thou art filled with shame for glory: drink thou also, and let thy foreskin be uncovered; the cup of the LORD'S right hand shall be turned unto thee, and shameful spewing shall be on thy glory.*

Somebody gets drunk in order to have some kind of sexual sin. Their will is broken down, and they fall into sinfulness. That's what happened to Noah.

Canaan Did It

I used to think, "But it was Ham who was cursed." But the Word never says that Ham was cursed . . . it says that *Canaan* (Ham's descendant) was cursed! Ham was the one who found his father in his drunken condition, but the curse didn't come on him because *he* didn't go into his father's tent and commit a homosexual act. *It was his son, Canaan, who did it*; and that's who the curse came upon. "The curse causeless does not come," and Canaan committed the sin.

For years people have said, "The black race is cursed because Ham was cursed, and Ham was black." That's such a lie of the devil! It's true that Ham was black—his name means *hot, or dark skinned*. But God didn't say, "Cursed be Ham." Whose name did He say? "Cursed be Canaan"! What color was Canaan? Canaan was white. So God didn't curse colors or races.

Don't say, "Well, I'm white, so I'm cursed." No, you're not

cursed because you're white. What did God curse? God cursed sin. If you get into sin, then you're cursed.

Canaan was cursed. Ham had four sons: Canaan, Mizraim, Phut, and Cush. Phut and Cush were the black sons, and they're the beginning of all the African tribes. Mizraim is the beginning of Egypt, and Egyptians are kind of beige-colored or olive-complected. But Canaan was white, the Canaanites were white, and all their descendants were white.

> *Thou shalt not bow down thyself to them, nor serve them; for I the LORD thy God am a jealous God, visiting the iniquity of the fathers upon the children unto the third and fourth generation of them that hate me* (Exodus 20:5).

Now if you follow this curse down—for the Bible says that this curse is visited to the fourth generation of those that hate Him—you can see how it came on the Canaanites' generations. When a father commits a sin, his son picks it up. There is a weakness already to sin, and the old nature which comes from the father is passed on to the son. Then the devil comes and tempts the son, and he falls into it too.

Sexual Sin Is the Worst

God destroyed Sodom and Gomorrah for what sin? Homosexuality. From whom did the inhabitants of Sodom and Gomorrah descend? They descended from Canaan. Canaan was the first homosexual, and that's what the people of Sodom and Gomorrah were involved in.

You can follow the Canaanites all the way through down to Joshua's day, and they were involved in sexual sins. They were into terrible things: homosexuality, lesbianism, sex with animals, sexual activity in front of idols. Yuck! They had every kind of perverted sex going on, and it's really too filthy even to mention.

But that's the kind of thing that went on with the Canaanites.

As those generations of sin go on, the sin gets worse in the people. The more people sin, the better they get at it. "Practice makes perfect"—only practicing sin makes something terrible.

There are curses that come down and attack a generation, and they have to be broken for them not to continue. You must break the family curse! You may have grandparents or parents or your children or yourself who is involved in all kinds of problems, but you don't have to be defeated by it! The devil would like to put that old family curse on you, but you can break its power over you and your family.

And if you resist it, he will try to put that thing on your children. Suddenly your children get wild at twelve or thirteen, and you think, "What happened to this sweet little thing?" Well, the devil came along and tempted your child with it. But it does not have to be that way!

The thing which provoked the curse in Noah's family was his own drunkenness. Noah got drunk, and that opened the way for sin. People believe drinking is such a little thing, but Proverbs 20:1 says, *"Wine is a mocker, strong drink is raging: and whosoever is deceived thereby is not wise."*

"Well, I drink a little wine for my stomach's sake." I doubt that you do it for your stomach. I think you drink a little wine for a buzz, or you do it to be accepted socially. But God says that wine is a mocker, and it's raging. Why? Because it brings a curse.

Proverbs 31:4-6 talks about leadership:

> *It is not for kings, O Lemuel, it is not for kings to drink wine; nor for princes strong drink: Lest they drink, and forget the law, and pervert the judgment of any of the afflicted. Give strong drink unto him that is ready to perish, . . .*

Leaders shouldn't drink—not even socially—because they never know when they're going to be called on to act in an emergency, and their actions can affect the whole nation.

There are two ways of looking at Proverbs 31:6, *"Give strong drink unto him that is ready to perish, . . . "* One is to say, "That man is dying. Give him a drink to revive him. Get his heart pumping and his breathing started again. Give him a drink to stimulate him." I guess that's not so bad, but there are better ways to perform C.P.R.!

The other way to understand Proverbs 31:6 is to say, "That man doesn't care much about life. Give him another drink so he'll slip into unconsciousness and eventually die. It looks like drinking has already killed his liver and his heart and his ambition, and there's not much left of him anyway. He's ready to give up and die, so let him have another drink." I pray that you'll never get to that point of self-destruction that you'll drink yourself to death. Either way, alcohol is not good for the healthy man!

Proverbs 23:20 says, *"Be not among winebibbers; among riotous eaters of flesh."* Don't even run around with people who drink.

Isaiah 5:11:

> *"Woe unto them that rise up early in the morning, that they may follow strong drink; that continue until night, till wine inflame them!"*

Why? What's going to happen if you continue to drink and drink and drink? Not only will it kill you, but what's worse, you will have put a curse on your family, your descendants.

"But where did I get this alcoholism from?" You may have gotten it from some long-ago relative, and the devil wants to pass that curse on to you.

Chapter Three

THE VALLEY OF BLESSING AND CURSING

Now turn to Deuteronomy 27 and 28. This is one of the most interesting portions in the Bible because it shows God's people putting His Word into action, comparing His blessings with some awful curses.

Before Moses turned the leadership of the children of Israel over to Joshua, he instructed them very carefully. Then, when Joshua took the Israelites into the Promised Land, they followed Moses' command and turned themselves into a "living Sunday school lesson."

Following Moses' instructions, Joshua divided all Israel into two groups. One group he sent over to Mount Gerizim, and the other group he sent over to Mount Ebal. To the priests or Levites in the first group, he gave a long list of blessings; and to the priests or Levites in the second group, he handed a long list of curses. Then Joshua conducted the two groups like an orchestra leader.

The first group shouted out the first blessing on their list, and the people answered, "Amen"—or "I understand." Then the second group shouted out their first curse, and the people answered, "Amen"—or "I agree." This went back and forth, and the people eventually had to decide which type they liked better, curses or blessings. Which kind would you choose?

> *And the Levites shall speak, and say unto all the men*
> *of Israel with a loud voice, Cursed be the man that*
> *maketh any graven or molten image, an abomination*
> *unto the LORD, . . .* (Deuteronomy 27:14,15).

So anybody who got involved in idolatry was in a cursed position. Idols bring curses. People who get involved in witchcraft or in a cult can pass that sin down from generation to generation.

The Witch's Curse

Once we saw a Baptist-made movie about a young man who was being witnessed to by a group of Christians. This young man wanted to be saved, but his mind was terribly attacked. It seemed that his grandmother was a witch, and she had put a curse on him. He couldn't receive the Lord because he was blinded by this curse.

But the Christians stood against the curse. Then the devil got mad and said, "I have killed the grandmother, and I've killed the mother in this family. Now I'm going to kill this boy." The evil spirit even said what time he was going to kill the boy.

The Christians continued to stand against the curse. They watched the clock, they spoke the Word against the curse, and they prayed. At the hour when the boy was supposed to die, the curse was broken, and he received Jesus as his Savior! Curses are awful, but they **can** be broken.

Different Curses

Back in the valley, there were curses on people who cursed their family:

> *"Cursed be he that setteth light by his father or his*
> *mother. And all the people shall say, Amen"*
> (Deuteronomy 27:16).

People who rebel against their parents bring a curse on

themselves, and that curse can be passed from generation to generation. Don't rebel against your parents. It doesn't matter what they're doing; you'll bring a curse upon yourself and pass it on to your children . . . and you don't want that to happen!

Then there is a curse of cruelty:

> *"Cursed be he that maketh the blind to wander out of the way. . . . "* (Deuteronomy 27:18).

There are people who are actually cruel and violent. I saw a television program about a mother who killed her own child, and I thought, "Oh, how terrible!" When they checked out that mother's background, they discovered she had been abused by *her* mother. She hadn't been killed by her mother, but the sin got worse as it progressed from one generation to the next. The mother had the weakness from her mother, and the evil spirits tempted her, and she fell in it, doing worse than had been done before.

Sexual sin seems to be one of the very worst curses. Deuteronomy 27:20-23 talks about all kinds of sexual sins that bring curses. People act like it's very funny to have an affair, but it's not so funny when the devil is robbing you of everything you've got, just throwing you down the drain. Immorality isn't funny at all. It's a curse; it's sin. It hurts you; it's desperate . . . and it will hurt your seed!

The last part of Deuteronomy 27 has to do with violence. Violence is a curse, and anyone who enjoys doing violence or watching violence or condoning violence is under a curse. Keep away from it! Don't promote it! And don't pass it on to your children.

In Deuteronomy 27 and 28, God told the Israelites what the curses were and what the blessings were. He said, "If you do these things, you're going to be cursed." He wanted the people to really be sure to get it, to have it tied into their hearts. So when they read the curses off, everybody said, "Amen." And when they read the blessings off, everybody said, "Amen."

The people didn't read it, but they heard it from the priests . . . and when they said "Amen" to it, they signified that they understood. God knew that these weaknesses from their past generations had to be broken. He knew they couldn't sow something evil into their children which would come up and be a curse back.

He not only wanted them to break the *past* generation curse, but He also wanted them to break the *present* generation curse. He says, "If you do righteously, you will be blessed. But if you do wrongly, you're going to bring the curses." So the people said "Amen" to it.

Written in Stone

The children of Israel were also to write down the blessings shouted down to them from Mount Gerizim, and they were to write down the curses shouted down to them from Mount Ebal. They wrote the blessings and curses down on stone, so they would never be forgotten, never be destroyed. As the people read the blessings and the curses, they answered, "Amen, amen, amen."

In other words, "If you want to be blessed, and if you want your seed to be blessed, don't get into sin, or you'll bring a curse. But if you do get into sin, this is what is going to happen to you. Do you understand?" The people answered, "Amen. Yes, we understand. We understand what the blessings will be, and we understand what the curses will be."

Fighting the Strong Man

Matthew 12:29 says:

> *"Or else how can one enter into a strong man's house, and spoil his goods, except he first bind the*

strong man? and then he will spoil his house."

In this scripture *house* can mean "generation" (see Matthew 10:6). In order to break the curse of the generations behind us—their habits, their sins, their physical weaknesses—you have to go in and bind the strong man who has brought that curse from generation to generation.

"So who is this 'strong man'?" Satan, of course. The devil is the strong man. "What do we have to do to him?" We must bind him. "And then what?" We take the *house*—or that generation—away from him!

We say, "Hey devil, wait a minute! My generation doesn't belong to you because I bind you in the name of Jesus, and you're not going to do it!" That's what we do; we break that curse in the name of Jesus.

When these awful things start to occur, we say, "I'm not going to have heart problems . . . I'm not going to have diabetes . . . I'm not going to be an alcoholic . . . I'm not going to have a weakness for immorality because my mother was involved in that . . . I'm not going to abuse my kids because I was beaten, or there was incest, or I was molested! That curse is not going to come on me. I'm not going to do it to my children, and my children are never going to do it to their children!"

Why? "Because I break that curse, and I bind that strong man. The curse of generations is broken!"

But if you think you're going to tell the devil to "get lost" just once, you're wrong! He'll come back and attack you again and again and again. You've got to get serious. Nobody ever said walking with the Lord and fighting with the devil is a cupcake! We need to be ready for spiritual warfare all the time!

This is an important lesson for young people. When the devil comes to you with immorality, that is a curse. Girls, when some guy wants something from you that you shouldn't be giving him, that's a curse. If you get into immorality, you will bring a curse on yourself, and on your children, and on your children's children. Don't do it. Don't get involved. Be smart.

Remember that the devil is trying to put a curse on you. You can say, "Hey, I'm not under the curse, I'm under the blood!" Head him off at the pass. Never get into it.

"Seven Other Spirits"

Now look at Matthew 12:43-45:

> *When the unclean spirit is gone out of a man, he walketh through dry places, seeking rest, and findeth none. Then he saith, I will return into my house from whence I came out; and when he is come, he findeth it empty, swept, and garnished. Then goeth he, and taketh with himself seven other spirits more wicked than himself, and they enter in and dwell there: and the last state of that man is worse than the first. Even so shall it be also unto this wicked generation.*

This is right in the same chapter as the other part about binding the strong man. When we defeat the devil the first time, we can be sure he's going to try again!

Here's what it says: *"When the unclean spirit is gone out of a man, he walketh through dry places, seeking rest, and findeth none."* So we see that the devil is cast out. *"Then he saith, I will return into my house . . . ."* Whose house? The devil thinks that *your house*—your generation, your seed, your children— belongs to him!

The devil thinks your children belong to him! You kicked him out, but he says, "I'll get your kids because that's my house, and I don't like walking around here in nothing. I've been in that generation—or I've been perpetuating that curse—for years and years, going way back. I don't like being kicked out of the family. I want to get back in the same family, so I'll just go after the kids."

That makes me so mad! The devil has the audacity to think that my house is his house! But my house does not belong to the devil. My house—my generation, my family, my children, my grandchildren—belongs to the Lord!

But what does the devil do? He's so mean and dirty that when he comes in, he finds it empty, swept, and garnished. You see, my house has been all cleaned up by Jesus. The Holy Spirit came in and threw out all the old junk and completely redecorated the whole place.

So what does the devil do then? He takes "*. . . seven other spirits more wicked than himself, and they enter in and dwell there; and the last state of that man is worse than the first. Even so shall it be also unto this wicked generation.*"

We're talking about generations, about families. The devil will come in and attack your children with the old weaknesses and the old sins that you had . . . or your grandmother had . . . or your great-grandmother had. He'll go after your kids, and they'll be worse than you were!

Why is this generation so bad? Sin is the worst we've ever seen it because the evil spirits have come with seven times more to attack. Whenever there has been a cleansing, they come after the kids to make them seven times worse. You'd better believe it: **the devil is after your children.** But he doesn't get them because *your house is not his house.* Don't you dare let him take them! Don't let your kids get into alcohol or drugs or immorality or any of that other garbage. Jesus came to set us free and to keep us free, and our houses belong to the Lord!

Chapter Four
THE MERCY SEAT

Now I'm going to give you some good news and some bad news. When we look at Noah's drunkenness, we say, "Oh, that is just so awful." What happened to Noah? He got drunk. But whenever there is sin—". . . *the curse causeless shall not come*" (Proverbs 26:2)—God makes a way to break that sin.

When Adam and Eve sinned, immediately God made a way to break that sin, to nullify that curse. Genesis 3:21 says:

"Unto Adam also and to his wife did the LORD God make coats of skins, and clothed them."

God killed an animal and made them coats of skin. He shed blood because *the blood was the answer to the curse!*

When Cain and Abel came upon the scene (Genesis 4), they knew what all had gone on before them. They knew about their parents' sin and how God's answer for their curse was the blood. But when it came time for the sons to make their own offerings, Cain ignored the blood and instead brought the vegetables which he grew. Abel brought a lamb from his flock because he knew that blood would break the curse.

Cain chose to ignore that there could be a curse for sin, just as there are people today who choose to ignore that sin can bring a curse. The devil tries to tell them, "Well, it might be a curse to so-and-so, but it won't hurt you. You're so sweet and good otherwise, what's one little sin?"

That's what Cain said: "I don't believe that I need to have the blood. I don't believe there is a curse." But his brother's sacrifice was accepted, and Cain's sacrifice was not accepted because he refused the blood. Similarly, if you refuse the truth, you'll believe a lie; you'll be deceived.

Cain was deceived, and he killed his brother. There is no answer for Cain because he refused the blood that he could have had. God *always* wants to break the curse with the blood!

What breaks the curse for you? The blood!

Whose blood? The blood of the Lamb!

What breaks the curse for your family? The blood!

What breaks the curse of inheriting bad things from the past? Absolutely, the blood of Jesus Christ!

Righteousness and Justice

God said, "When you bring the blood, you get mercy from the curse." Adam and Eve and their children had a place to worship the Lord. They were outside the Garden, but they had a special place where there were two cherubs. This was a foreshadowing of the Mercy Seat. These two cherubs mean *righteousness* and *justice*.

When they brought the blood of the lamb and sprinkled it on the Mercy Seat, they said, "God won't judge us because He sees the blood, and the blood breaks the curse of our sin." That was an example of the Mercy Seat.

Then there was the first physical Mercy Seat. In Exodus 25 and 26, God told Moses how to make the tabernacle: "Put the Ark of the Covenant in the Holy of Holies, and it will have a big golden lid; and it will have two cherubims, and they will face each other . . . when the high priest goes in on the Day of Atonement, he will sprinkle blood on the Mercy Seat."

By this, God says, "Instead of judging your sins, they are judged through the blood sacrifice. I will break the curse through the blood. Justice and righteousness are satisfied by the blood."

Now let's go to Jesus. Jesus arose from the dead. The disciples looked in His tomb, and they saw two angels, one at the head where His body lay and one at the foot. What was that indicating? *Jesus is our Mercy Seat. He shed His blood to break the curse!* All righteousness and justice is satisfied because of the blood of Jesus.

There is no reason for us to take a curse physically, mentally, emotionally, or in any way from a past generation or relationship. Thank God, we're free!

According to Hebrews 9:14, Jesus took His blood up to the Father. Everything which was on earth as "the Tabernacle" was patterned after the heavenly (Hebrews 9:23). Jesus took His blood and put it upon the Mercy Seat in heaven. He said, "Father, here is My blood."

The Father replied, "Here is the Mercy Seat. All who come under Your blood are already judged."

Now, anyone who has taken my Bible school course knows that when I give a test, there are 100 points on it, and you have to get at least 60 correct to pass. But when you take a test from God, if you miss one, you fail. When you sin one time, you're as much of a sinner as the guy who sinned a million times. You failed the test, so you get the curse.

But then Jesus came down and said, "I'll take the test for you." What did Jesus score on that test? He got one hundred percent! So when you meet up with the devil, you give him Jesus' test score and say, "He took the test. I'm in Him; I have His blood, and it speaks of better things. It breaks your curse, so beat it!"

The Curse of the Canaanites

There are some people who broke the curse. When we looked at Noah and his lineage, we saw that Cain's seed kept getting into sin. There was Lamech and a whole bunch of bad people in his seed. The sin came down in those generations, and nobody broke it with the blood.

Noah was forgiven of his drunkenness because he made a sacrifice. He took the blood, and the blood spoke mercy, and that satisfied righteousness and justice for what he had done.

But look at those Canaanites. They're so bad. They kept getting into sin, and those evil spirits were attacking each generation, saying, "That's my house! That's my house!" It's getting worse and worse and worse.

"How did they get out of sin?" Well, they **did** get out of sin, but not in a good way.

God told Joshua, "When you go in to take Canaan, kill them all. I don't want any of them because there are so many generations of sin, and it has to be broken. Sin is contagious, and I don't want it catching onto you."

They were Cain's cursed generations. Noah had stopped the curse, but Canaan revived it. So finally God decided to kill all the Canaanites when their iniquity was "full" (Genesis 15:16). God told Joshua to do it. It was God's command: "Kill them all."

Why? Maybe they had AIDS. I wouldn't be surprised because if they had homosexuality, lesbianism, sexual activity with animals, and all that garbage for generation after generation, who knows what disease they must have had by this time!

Twenty-four thousand Israelites got involved with the Midianites, and they all died in a day. Their sin was a very serious thing. Sin brings a curse.

Joshua and the Israelites were ready to go into the Promised Land and kill all the Canaanites at God's command. But there was a woman named Rahab, who was a Canaanite and a prostitute. She had all kinds of sexual sins—all of that sin inherited from generation to generation. But somehow she got ahold of God's Word, she believed it, and broke the curse!

> *"Know therefore that the LORD thy God, he is God, the faithful God, which keepeth covenant and mercy with them that love him and keep his commandments to a thousand generations"* (Deuteronomy 7:9).

Not only did she break the curse for herself—she broke it for her future generations. *"They that love Me, I will bless them to one thousand generations."*

That means you say to the devil, "You don't get my children, you don't get my grandchildren, you don't get my great-grandchildren. If Jesus tarries, you don't get anyone who belongs to my house for a thousand generations! This curse will not go on. It will stop in Jesus' name."

That's how Rahab stopped the curse. "How do you know that God blessed her future?" Rahab married a Jew, and she had a baby. She named that baby Boaz. Boaz married Ruth, who became the mother of Obed. Obed had a son named Jesse; Jesse had a son named David, and David became the king. Rahab is in the lineage of Jesus Christ! Is that blessed enough?

We can go down a thousand generations and see Rahab as blessed. What was her past? A Canaanite and a prostitute . . . but the blood was satisfied, and the curse was broken!

When the Israelites came in to fight the Gibeonites, there was a similar story (Joshua 9 and 10). The Gibeonites were Canaanites, but they came under the blood. They were deceivers, rapists, liars; even their name means "a snake." But they said, "We want your God." When they did that, they broke the curse.

Ruth was another example. She was a Moabitess, one of the worst kind. Her genealogy was terrible. But when she came to the Lord, what happened? She came under the blood sacrifice, and the blood broke the curse. The blood can break any curse.

The Name Above All Names

. . . Blessed be the LORD God of Shem; . . . God shall enlarge Japheth, and he shall dwell in the tents of Shem; and Canaan shall be his servant (Genesis 9:26,27).

"Oh, poor Noah. That grandson of his, Canaan, produced such a bad line." But there were three sons: Ham, Shem, and Japheth. Of Shem the Bible says, "He will have a tent, and they will come under his tent." ". . . *Blessed be the LORD God of Shem; . . . God shall enlarge Japheth, and he shall dwell in the tents of Shem; and Canaan shall be his servant.*"

This means that both brothers and all their descendants will come under Shem's tent, or be covered and protected by him. Of course, Ham's descendants—Canaan and his seed—will be servants to Shem's descendants because of the curse, and not equals or inheritors of the blessing.

Shem means "name." What was Noah actually prophesying when he said, "They will come under Shem's tent"? He was saying, "They will be protected by Shem . . . or by the *name.*"

The Jewish race came through the descendants of Shem. Noah was saying, "There will be a *name* that even Canaan can run under and find protection!" And who would be the name that would come through Shem? Who is their very own Messiah? Who is the name above all names? **Jesus!** Jesus became a curse that we might be blessed!

When something rises up in your household, you need to rebuke that curse. Then you should tell your children, "I've blown it; I've sinned. That's a curse, but the devil is not going to put it on you. I've repented of it. I've received mercy and righteousness through the blood of Jesus. Now don't you get into the same curse just because I did. You are saved from the curse!"

You can make the decision just where your lineage is going to go. They are going to go for Jesus . . . or they are going to go for the devil. The devil is after your family, but you can stop him before he ever starts!

Once we cast an evil spirit out of a woman. We asked the evil spirit, "When did you go in there?" He told us some junky thing. Then we asked, "Why are you in there?"

The evil spirit answered, "Because if I get her, I get her kid too." The devil doesn't tell the truth very often, but I think he told it right then.

We rebuked that spirit, saying, "You don't get her kids because you don't get her!" That woman was delivered. Six or seven years later she came to our church.

She said to me, "I'm Bonnie. Do you remember me?"

I answered, "Do I remember you! I'll never forget you!" She was my first experience with casting out demons! Glory to God—we broke that generation curse!

She said, "We belong to Jesus, and He belongs to us, and so does our family!"

Terry's Story

There was a man in our church who had a terrible background of alcoholism. Terry's testimony is beautiful. I'll let him tell it in his own words:

37

"In our family there were five boys. Including my dad, all the men were alcoholics. Dad was from Hazard, Kentucky, where you either worked in the coal mines or sold moonshine for a living. My father drank vodka for fifty years; but during the last year of his life, all Dad wanted to do was watch preachers on TV and go home to be with Jesus.

"I never lived too long with my oldest brother, Darrell. He was a lot older than me. When I was only about 4 or 5 years old, he was already an alcoholic. I remember when I was little, watching him knife-fight out behind the house in an alley. But when I saw him a year ago, I sat down and talked with him. All Darrell wants to talk about is what God is doing in his life. There is nothing else important to him.

"My next brother—who is four years older than me—was an alcoholic who went over to Vietnam. When he came back, all he did was drink. But the last time I saw him, he had married a Pentecostal preacher's daughter from Middletown, Ohio, and now they take turns preaching on Sunday.

"I've got a brother a year older than me. He had a pretty rough time of it. He couldn't escape with drinking. God is really working in his life; we've seen a lot of things break off of him. He's going to heaven too, but he just doesn't know it yet.

"I went in the hospital about six years ago. I was so drunk when we filled out the (admission) papers that I didn't even know what year I was born or whether I was married or not.

"A nurse took me aside one night and said, 'Now, Terry, you've just got one chance. When was the last time you prayed?'

"'It's been a long time ago,' I answered.

"'Why don't you pray now?' she asked. For about fifteen or twenty minutes, I told her how I wasn't good enough to ask God for help. She said, 'You tell your Father that, and know the God of your understanding' (Exodus 35:31).

"I answered, 'Well, I can do that.' So I went into my room, got down on my knees, and told God how I wasn't good enough. I said, 'You can take me if You want to. I don't want any half-way job done.

"'But if You do take me, I'll do what You say from here on out.' I ended that prayer the way I had been taught: 'In the power of Jesus' name.'

"'I got up off my knees knowing that I was never going to drink again. I knew it then, and I haven't drank another drop since then, not in six years.

"You might be somebody who was as sick as I was. You don't have to drink anymore if you're willing to let God run your life daily. I've talked with people who are alcoholics, and people who have grown up in homes with alcoholics. There are even people who've been coming to church for five, ten, twenty years, and you know that you've got a bottle rattling back there.

"Maybe you've been drinking since you were a kid, or maybe it's somebody in your family or one of your kids who drinks. If God has been dealing with you about drinking for a long time, don't be deceived. The devil isn't that strong; we give him more power than he deserves.

"The other kind of person is one who has grown up in an alcoholic home, or has married an alcoholic and later divorced or something. You're doing all you can do to walk with the Lord and do His ways. But there is always something there that just keeps at you and keeps at you, and you can't figure out what it is. Don't be deceived any longer. God has got a plan for you too.

"My family once lifted up a vegetable in prayer—me—and stood on the Word of God, and I came back as a complete miracle! I am the result of prayer. My whole family is a miracle! We were *all* alcoholics . . . and now we're all saved."

Breaking the Curse of Alcohol

Before you read any further, if you, like Terry, are fighting an alcohol problem that goes back generation after generation, stop right now and pray aloud this prayer:

"Dear heavenly Father, You love me! You sent Your Son to break this curse from my past generation and from me. This alcoholic curse is going to stop this very moment. Never again will I have this problem.

"I give this alcoholism to Jesus. Jesus set me free! He took the test for me, and He passed one hundred percent. So I have His test score. I have His name, and I run under that name. That name covers me. That blood cleanses me right now, and I am free by the blood. In the name of Jesus, amen."

Now make this declaration of faith out loud:

"Satan! You and your evil spirits of alcoholism have heard my prayer right now! You've had your chance, but your power is broken. Never again will I—nor anyone in my house—ever be a slave to alcohol. In Jesus' name, your curse is broken. Your interference in my life is stopped right now.

"I once was an alcoholic, but now I am delivered. The family curse is broken. My children, and my grandchildren, and my great-grandchildren—no one in my family—will ever be an alcoholic because the blood of Jesus Christ has cleansed us today and for always. So, devil, get out of here!"

When you've finished your confession of faith, remember to thank and praise Jesus often for His blood and His deliverance. And be faithful to tell others where your "cure" from alcoholism came from!

Chapter Five

INHERITED CURSES

Curses are transmitted from generation to generation. Secular insurance companies know this. That's why they ask, "Is there a history of heart disease in your family? Is there kidney failure? High blood pressure? Diabetes?" Exodus 20:5 says the sins of the fathers are visited on the children, down to the fourth generation.

That used to bother me terribly. I thought, "Now wait a minute! I don't want to have to answer for my great-grandfather's sin!" It's enough to answer for and deal with your own sins.

But there is a law in nature, called the "law of culpability." The dictionary defines *culpability* as "responsibility for wrong or error; blameworthy" (American Heritage Dictionary, 1976).

The scripture says that every man shall answer for his own sin. They will be accountable to God for their sins, but that weakness in an area of their lives—physically, mentally, emotionally—is transmitted to the next generation, or maybe the generation after that. That's what is so bad. And it's because "... *of them that hate me*" (Exodus 20:5).

Let's review a little. Deuteronomy 27 and 28 tells us all about the curses and the blessings. As the curses were read out, everybody—the men, the women, the children, the grandmothers and grandfathers—heard them, and they answered, "Amen, so be it." God wanted them to know that sin brings

41

a curse. He wasn't trying to be hard on them. He wanted to be good to them so they wouldn't bring curses on their lives.

Proverbs 26:2 says, " . . . *the curse causeless shall not come*"—or, "When there is a curse on a generation, it didn't just happen to occur; there has to be a cause behind it." What is always the cause behind the curse? Sin. Sin is what always brings the curse. Any time there is a curse in a person's life, there is some root of sin.

When I visited with my aunt, another thing I asked her was, "What was my grandfather like?"

She answered, "Let me tell you about your great-grandfather first. He would go on a drunk once a year, and then he would beat his animals. There were a lot of good things about him, but there was one bad thing: he was cruel to his animals."

Then she went on to say that my grandfather had that same kind of cruelty. In my family, we've seen that cruelty occur again and again. Cruelty is a curse. When you are being cruel or unkind or hateful to somebody, you are in a cursed area.

Deuteronomy 27 talks about sexual sins. God comes down harder on sexual sins than anything else. Adultery, fornication, lesbianism, homosexuality . . . these are heavy-duty curses because they are heavy-duty sins.

Violence is another curse. Any time we see violence coming down through generations—first a man who's very cruel, then his daughter, then his grandson, then his great-grandchildren— you know they are under a terrible curse. Sometimes a curse can skip a generation, and then when it shows up later, people wonder, "Where did that terrible thing come from?"

But God came to make the terrible into the beautiful, and He came to reverse the curse. We have to look at the curse in order to get free from it.

Droughts and Diseases

The LORD shall make the pestilence cleave unto thee, until he have consumed thee from off the land, whither thou goest to possess it. The LORD shall smite thee with a consumption, and with a fever, and with an inflammation, and with an extreme burning, and with the sword, and with blasting, and with mildew; and they shall pursue thee until thou perish (Deuteronomy 28:21,22).

Disease, and your enemy coming after you, would be a part of sin. When you sin, when you disobey, you break the law, and then the curse is going to be there.

Then God talks about drought, a lack of rain:

And thy heaven that is over thy head shall be brass, and the earth that is under thee shall be iron. The LORD shall make the rain of thy land powder and dust: from heaven shall it come down upon thee, until thou be destroyed (Deuteronomy 28:23,24).

He was saying, "If you go into idolatry and get into sin, you will cause drought and famine."

When the Israelites got into idolatry under Ahab and Jezebel, Elijah prayed, "God, don't let it rain for three-and-a-half years." When the people repented, the fire from heaven fell. Then Elijah prayed, and he watched and waited . . . and the rain came. Why? When the people repented, they reversed the curse. The way to break the curse is by repentance.

Now how did Elijah stop the rain from falling in the first place? He used the Scriptures. He didn't get mad at Ahab and Jezebel, and just spitefully say, "I'm going to stop it from raining." He simply prayed the Word of God:

> *" . . . As the* LORD *God of Israel liveth, before whom*
> *I stand, there shall not be dew nor rain these years,*
> *but according to my word"* (I Kings 17:1).

He said, "I've gone to the Word," and he prayed the Word, and he stopped the rain. Then he prayed the Word and broke the curse because the people repented, and the rain came again:

> *Then there was a famine in the days of David three*
> *years, year after year; and David enquired of the*
> LORD. *And the* LORD *answered, It is for Saul, and*
> *for his bloody house, because he slew the Gibeonites.*
> *Wherefore David said unto the Gibeonites, What*
> *shall I do for you? and wherewith shall I make the*
> *atonement, that ye may bless the inheritance of the*
> LORD? (II Samuel 21:1,3).

After the death of Saul, there was a drought that went on for years. David went to God and asked, "What's wrong, Lord? This is not a natural drought, so what is wrong?"

God answered, "It is because Saul killed innocent Gibeonites. That blood calls for vengeance; that has to be taken care of."

So David went to the Gibeonites and asked, "What shall we do? Saul's house had something wrong, and we're suffering for it. There is a curse because of his sin."

What brought the curse? Sin. A curse doesn't just happen, it just doesn't come wandering along and attach itself to you. It always comes because of sin. And just like His instructions to Joshua, God said, "You have to cleanse the earth."

David asked the Gibeonites how to break the curse. They said, "Well, let the leftover relatives of Saul be hung." In order for the curse on Saul's house to be broken, the rest of the family had to be wiped out.

They found five of Saul's grandchildren, and his two sons

by Rizpah, and they hanged them. This made the Gibeonites happy, because their "innocent dead" were now avenged.

But do you remember Rizpah? Her name means "hot rock." She warms your heart by what she did! The curse of Saul's generations was now broken, but there was still shame and mourning in his family. So Rizpah "demonstrated." She went to the execution site and covered the bodies of the seven hanged men with her robe. Then she sat out on the rocks by the bodies in the open air and mourned publicly until David took notice of her grief.

Then David decided to honor the dead of the royal house of Saul. He gathered all their bones—and brought the bones of Saul and Jonathan too—and buried them all with honors in their family tomb. He laid that family to rest once and for all!

Hereditary Illnesses and Problems

Heredity: "The genetic transmission of characteristics from parent to offspring; the totality of characteristics and associated potentialities transmitted to an individual by heredity" (American Heritage Dictionary, 1976).

There are generations of families who suffer nothing but defeat. Wally and I know a family where the grandfather was defeated, the father is defeated, and the two children of that family are defeated. One of the children died of cancer, and the other son is so fearful. I hate to think what will happen to the grandchildren and on down. That would be the fourth generation visited with that same curse. That's awful.

There are certain family diseases:

> *The LORD will smite thee with the botch of Egypt, and with the emerods, and with the scab, and with the itch, whereof thou canst not be healed. The LORD shall smite thee with madness, and blindness,*

and astonishment of heart (Deuteronomy 28:27,28).

The botch of Egypt is boils and tumors; tumors are a form of cancer. Madness and astonishment of heart are confusion of mind and amnesia; these are mental illnesses.

Blindness is glaucoma, cataracts, near-sightedness and far-sightedness and all the eye diseases. Have you ever seen a family where every single one of them wears glasses? From the father and mother down to the littlest child, all are wearing glasses, and usually those really thick-lensed kind. Those poor people are under a curse, and they need to be set free from it!

Then God talks about poverty:

> . . . *thou shalt not prosper in thy ways: and thou shalt be only oppressed and spoiled evermore, and no man shall save thee. Thou shalt betroth a wife, and another man shall lie with her: thou shalt build an house, and thou shalt not dwell therein: thou shalt plant a vineyard, and shalt not gather the grapes thereof* (Deuteronomy 28:29,30).

"Well, I come from a family where nobody knows how to handle their finances. No one ever taught me how to save money or to tithe or to be thrifty." We're talking about more than just careless habits or a lack of sound teaching—we're talking about being under a curse!

Another current example of the curse of poverty is the huge number of home repossessions going on in today's economy:

> " . . . *thou shalt build an house, and thou shalt not dwell therein:* . . . " (verse 30).

The curse just gets worse and worse, from generation to generation.

And in lower income families, immorality is rampant:

*"Thou shalt betroth a wife, and another man shall
lie with her: . . . "* (verse 30).

Here's what happens: the alcoholic father takes his paycheck
to the closest bar and drinks it all away. So his wife starts fooling
around with the next door neighbor man because her husband
is never home anyway.

Then there's a divorce, the abandoned wife is left with all
the children, and rarely does she get any child support. Those
children grow up with their mothers having one boyfriend after
another, and they hardly know who their father is.

Poverty breeds immorality, shame, carelessness, and crime.
The curse starts in one generation and just grows and grows,
making itself worse with each new generation. Where did that
curse come from? "The curse causeless shall not come." There
must have been sin!

Familiar Spirits

Remember what we read in Matthew 12:29 and 43-45 about
the "strong man" and the "seven wicked spirits"? The Hebrew
word for *house* is translated "generation" or "family lines":

*"When the unclean spirit is gone out of a man . . . he
findeth it empty, swept, and garnished"* (verses 43,44).

This means that you get born again, and you're filled with
the Spirit. You have a new life in you, you have a new nature
in you. But your children can inherit your weakness!

Your generation has been cleansed, but your children have
got to walk in cleansing too! The curse has to be broken from
them too, or they will inherit the weaknesses from you which
came from your father and back from your grandfather and
your great-grandfather. What does the devil do? He watches
for those new generations so he can attack them too. He
watches at their birth.

"Marilyn, how do you know that?" Because the Old Testament talks about "familiar spirits":

> *"Regard not them that have familiar spirits . . . to be defiled by them: I am the LORD your God"* (Leviticus 19:31).

> *And the soul that turneth after such as have familiar spirits, . . . I will even set my face against that soul, and will cut him off from among his people* (Leviticus 20:6).

What are "familiar spirits"? They are fallen evil spirits that become familiar with a family. They follow that family with its weaknesses—physical, mental, emotional sin—all the way down, attacking and tempting each member in that way because they already know that they have a weakness for it.

If your father was an alcoholic, those evil spirits will watch you. They know that you probably already inherited a weakness for alcohol, and they'll drive you crazy. If you have children, they'll watch for the next generation, to attack them too. They are familiar with your family from generation to generation, and they try to get each generation into sin so they can carry the curse on from there.

Saul and the Witch of En-dor

An example of familiar spirits is given in the account of the witch of En-dor (I Samuel 28). Saul went to this witch because he had totally blown it with God. He had sinned, and he had not repented. He could have reversed his curse if he had admitted his sins to God.

God could have turned his situation around . . . the same with Cain, the same with Esau. But they didn't repent of their sins; it was always somebody else's fault. With Saul, "It was David's fault" . . . with Esau, "It was Jacob's fault" . . . with Cain, "It was Abel's fault." They didn't get their cleansings because they were too busy doing their cop-outs!

And when Saul saw the host of the Philistines, he was afraid, and his heart greatly trembled. And when Saul enquired of the LORD, the LORD answered him not, neither by dreams, nor by Urim, nor by prophets. Then said Saul unto his servants, Seek me a woman that hath a familiar spirit, that I may go to her, and enquire of her. And his servants said to him, Behold, there is a woman that hath a familiar spirit at En-dor. And Saul disguised himself, and put on other raiment, and he went, and two men with him, and they came to the woman by night: and he said, I pray thee, divine unto me by the familiar spirit, and bring me him up, whom I shall name unto thee.

Then said the woman, Whom shall I bring up unto thee? And he said, Bring me up Samuel. And when the woman saw Samuel, she cried with a loud voice . . . And the king said unto her, Be not afraid: for what sawest thou? And the woman said unto Saul, I saw gods ascending out of the earth. And he said unto her, What form is he of? And she said, An old man cometh up; and he is covered with a mantle. And Saul perceived that it was Samuel . . . And Samuel said to Saul. Why hast thou disquieted me, to bring me up?

Because thou obeyedst not the voice of the LORD, nor executedst his fierce wrath upon Amalek, therefore hath the LORD done this thing unto thee this day. Moreover the LORD will also deliver Israel with thee into the hand of the Philistines: and to morrow shalt thou and thy sons be with me: the LORD also shall deliver the host of Israel into the hand of the Philistines (I Samuel 28:5-8,11-15,18-19).

Saul couldn't face the truth, and he was deceived. If you refuse the truth, you will believe a lie. He went to see the witch at En-dor to find out if he was going to win the battle or not. The witch called up a spirit, but I do not believe that it was Samuel.

It looked like Samuel, it talked like Samuel, it had a mantle like Samuel's. It said, "Why did you cause me unrest? I was very much at peace. I'm going to tell you what's going to happen to you. Tomorrow you and your household are going to be killed."

Witches don't call us out of graves. Jesus does. He called Lazarus back from the grave (John 11). He brings the resurrection. But the evil spirit who had the appearance of Samuel was a familiar spirit. "How could that evil spirit emulate Samuel so well?" Because it was familiar with Samuel and his family.

There are all sorts of occult practices today. There are people who find somebody who is grieving over losing a loved one, and they will say, "Come in, and we will call that loved one." They knock on tables and do all kinds of funny things. Then some strange evil spirit enters and says, "I'm Uncle Joe. How are you doing? I'm missing you too."

Well, it's not Uncle Joe. Those people cannot bring up the spirits of real people. So what is that spirit? It is an evil spirit that is familiar with Uncle Joe.

If you're doing this sort of thing—playing with Ouija boards and such—then you're involved with a dangerous thing. Flee from anything like that. You do not need to be around familiar spirits or evil spirits. You need to be around the Holy Spirit constantly. And you need to warn your children about it. They should not have any part with it.

Chapter Six

THE CURSE OF THE HERODS

Herod the Great

Now when Jesus was born in Bethlehem of Judaea in the days of Herod the king, behold, there came wise men from the east to Jerusalem, Saying, Where is he that is born King of the Jews? for we have seen his star in the east, and are come to worship him. When Herod the king had heard these things, he was troubled, and all Jerusalem with him (Matthew 2:1-3).

Now this is Herod "the Great." Herod the Great was not Jewish, but he wasn't totally something else either. He was an Idumean, which is an Edomite; an Edomite is a descendant of Esau. So he was of a cursed generation because Esau hated the things of God (Genesis 25:34; Hebrews 12:16,17).

When you follow the history of the Edomites, they hated the things of God too. They were always bugging the Israelites, and there was never a good feeling between these "cousins." History records that the sons of Esau hated God, and the sons of Jacob loved God. There was a battle between them.

Herod the Great was half Idumean and half Jewish. Within his own nature there was a battle between the God-lovers and the God-haters. But Herod was being dealt with by God. God always wants to break the generation curse; that is always His will. So He sent the Word and the witness of someone to break that sin, to absolutely snap it around.

In this case God sent the wise men to Herod, and they told him about this star. So Herod went to his scribes and asked, "Can you find anything out that would help me to know if this really is the king of the Jews?"

This is a very supernatural dealing. Those wise men were not Jews; they're not Idumeans. They've come from the Far East, and, supernaturally, an unusual star has appeared. They are following that star, just as it had been prophesied by Balaam:

> *I shall see him, but not now: I shall behold him, but not nigh: there shall come a Star out of Jacob, and a Sceptre shall rise out of Israel, and shall smite the corners of Moab, and destroy all the children of Sheth. And Edom shall be a possession, Seir also shall be a possession for his enemies; and Israel shall do valiantly* (Numbers 24:17,18).

So the wise men come to Herod the Great, and this is a very supernatural sign. What do you think is happening to Herod? "Somebody is knocking at his door." Who is it? "God is knocking at his door." Any time there is a supernatural sign, or a miracle comes into your life from the hand of God, He is trying to get your attention.

The scribes looked it up in the Scriptures. They said, "Yeah, in the Word it says Somebody is to be born in Bethlehem and that He is to be the king." So they gave Herod the Word.

Any time the Word comes, what does it bring? "The Word brings light." What is happening to the darkness of this man? "The light of the Word of God is knocking at his door."

But what did Herod do with the light? He refused it. He had the opportunity to have the curse of his generations broken, but he rejected it!

He had generation after generation of curses and sin that he had inherited, but he blew his chance to be set free from the curse. Then he turned and committed an even worse sin, the really terrible mass murder of all the little male babies under two years of age.

Herod Antipas

Now Herod the Great had a son: Herod Antipas. All of his sons had the generation curse on them because the sins of the fathers are now visited on the children (Exodus 34:7). There was a weakness in Herod Antipas. But God always wants to break a curse. It doesn't matter what the weakness is, it doesn't matter how bad the sin is, because repentance and the blood of Jesus will break the curse!

God began to deal with Herod Antipas (Mark 6:14-28). Herod had committed a very bad sin: he had married his brother Philip's wife, Herodias. John the Baptist preached against it, saying that it was wrong.

So Herodias had a fit, and said, "Throw him in prison! I don't like him talking about me on the streets!" John probably called her a prostitute and harlot. So they threw him in jail:

> For Herod feared John, knowing that he was a just man and an holy, and observed him; and when he heard him, he did many things, and heard him gladly (Mark 6:20).

But Herod Antipas was touched by John. He called John up out of prison and said, "John, talk to me about spiritual things." Herod was hungry! So John talked to him, and you could see that Herod's heart was being turned.

What is God getting ready to do? Break the curse! John gave Herod the Word . . . the Word brought light . . . the light began to chase away the darkness. God's light is greater than any generation curse.

But one night Herodias had a big birthday party for Herod, and it was a drunken brawl. She brought out her glamorous daughter, Salome—who was not Herod's daughter, but was his niece—who began to dance before him. Herod was very much aroused by this girl, and he said, "I'll give you anything to the half of my kingdom."

So Salome ran to her mother and said, "What shall I ask?"

Well, Herodias was mad. She answered, "You bring me John the Baptist's head, that's what I want." So Herod Antipas had to stick to his promise, and he cut off John the Baptist's head. He really felt bad about it. But instead of letting the light overcome the darkness, he kept on in the curse. He was acting in violence and cruelty, just like his father.

But God didn't stop dealing with him. If it were me, I'd throw some of these people out the window! I wouldn't be like God and try again. I'd say, "Forget it. They're all a mess!" But God isn't like that. He keeps trying to break that family generation curse. So Jesus appeared before Herod Antipas.

By this time, Herod Antipas was a nervous wreck. When Jesus was brought before him (Luke 9:9 and 23:8-11), Herod—still feeling guilty—said, "Oh, are you John the Baptist risen from the dead?" When Jesus—the beautiful Savior of mankind and the world—came to Herod, he refused Him, and so that curse was not broken.

Herod Agrippa

Now about that time Herod the king stretched forth his hands to vex certain of the church. And he killed James the brother of John with the sword. And because he saw it pleased the Jews, he proceeded further to take Peter also. (Then were the days of unleavened bread.) And when he had apprehended him, he put him in prison, and delivered him to four quaternions of soldiers to keep him; intending after Easter to bring him forth to the people. Peter therefore was kept in prison: but prayer was made without ceasing of the church unto God for him (Acts 12:1-5).

I would have said, "Forget it. Hang it up." But God kept trying for four generations! So here is another Herod, the third one. This one threw Peter in jail, and he was going to kill him. The Jews were very happy that Peter was in jail, and Herod had already killed James.

Herod was thrilled and thought this added to his popularity contest. He was very aware of politics, and evidently he was not too popular. But while Peter was in jail, watch God deal with this Herod.

God sent an angel who released Peter, and Herod heard of this tremendous miracle. All these miracles have been happening in the city anyway, and he knew about them. Any time there is the miraculous, God is trying to deal with people. God gets a lot of mileage out of a miracle. He is trying to deal with this Herod to repent.

But this Herod—instead of repenting—murdered the men who were guards for Peter. He refused the light, holding onto the violence and cruelty which he got from his grandfather and his father. There is that curse, and "the curse causeless does not come," does it? But the curse can be broken.

Herod Agrippa II

And as he thus spake for himself, Festus said with a loud voice, Paul, thou art beside thyself; much learning doth make thee mad. But he said, I am not

> *mad, most noble Festus; but speak forth the words*
> *of truth and soberness. For the king knoweth of these*
> *things, before whom also I speak freely: for I am*
> *persuaded that none of these things are hidden from*
> *him; for this thing was not done in a corner. King*
> *Agrippa, believest thou the prophets? I know that*
> *thou believest. Then Agrippa said unto Paul, Almost*
> *thou persuadest me to be a Christian* (Acts 26:24-28).

The next generation of Herods was Herod Agrippa II, and we read about him in Acts 25 and 26. He was the great-grandson of Herod the Great. Herod Agrippa II was called to listen to a man in a courtroom scene. What's the man's name? "Paul the Apostle." Now God is sending them the best of His warriors!

Paul was brought before Agrippa II and said, "King Agrippa, I know you're not ignorant of things." So Herod Agrippa must have been stirred and drawn of God. God wanted to break this thing once and for all and get those evil spirits out of that generation curse. He wanted to turn a whole family around, a family that was making a tremendous impression on their whole nation.

Perhaps the saddest words in the Bible are when Paul preached to Agrippa, and his reply was, "Paul, you almost persuaded me." "Almost" is not enough. You are fully persuaded—or you're not in. Herod Agrippa II lost it, and he was the fourth generation.

Herod Agrippa II was the last of his family. They were the rulers of their country, but they lost it all. History says that Agrippa lost his position and bought a farm on Mount Vesuvius, to live out the rest of his life in shame and exile. But Mount Vesuvius was a bad place to buy a farm because when it erupted and destroyed all the countryside, that was the end of the Herods.

God wanted to break that family curse all the way down. He dealt with each Herod, and each one rejected Him. He tried with the first generation, and the second, and the third, and the fourth. The sins of the fathers were being visited on the children for four generations, and God tried to break the curse at each generation.

Now think about it: have you ever heard or read of another Herod? You never hear about Herod today. You've never met anybody who said, "I'm from those famous Herods back there in Jesus' day." Why? Because they perished; there are no Idumeans (or Edomites) today because they were devoured by the curse. The devil wants to do the same to *your* family line, but God has provided the way to stop the curse and replace it with blessing!

Chapter Seven

FAMILY CURSES AND BLESSINGS

God Blessed the Family

God has always been concerned about the family. In Genesis, He established four divine institutions:

1. The first one is free will (Genesis 2:16). God made man with free will.

2. The second institution was marriage (Genesis 2:18,21-25). God has always meant for us to marry.

3. The third was the family (Genesis 3:16, 4:1,2). God made marriage to be the nest to protect the children, where children are trained so they will go out and reproduce and raise their children to become Christians to continue from there.

4. The fourth was nations (Genesis 11:6-9). After the flood God never intended for just one nation to rule the whole world. He intended that there would always be small nations because they would protect individual rights.

God has such unique things planned for the family! He put His blessing on Adam and Eve, and He gave them and their children dominion. But they sinned, and sin brings the curse.

As soon as they sinned, God brought a way out of the sin:

through the shedding of blood, He clothed them with animals (Genesis 3:21). Right away, they saw there was a way out from the curse, and they had access to His Mercy Seat.

Esau Blew It

God then began to show Abraham how He would bless the family (Genesis 13:14-16). He said, "I'm really going to bless your seed." God gave Abraham tremendous promises for his seed. When Isaac came on the scene, He really blessed the family. Then Jacob came on the scene, and He blessed the family. But Esau blew it:

> *Also Esau saw that the daughters of Canaan did not please Isaac his father. So Esau went to Ishmael, and took to be his wife, [in addition] to the wives he [already] had, Mahalath daughter of Ishmael Abraham's son, the sister of Nebaioth* (Genesis 28:8,9 Amplified).

I've always thought, "Well, Esau blew it because he sold his birthright. He treated the things of God lightly and never did repent of what he had done. Oh sure, he was sorry about the situation—and he wanted to kill Jacob for what he'd done—but he never repented of his own sin. He just got into vengeance."

But there's something else that Esau did. He married Hittites. Esau had two Hittite wives.

"What's so bad about that?"

Isaac and Rebecca were very grieved over Esau's marrying those two women. They had sent Jacob up to Laban to get a wife, but what was the problem with Esau getting Hittite wives?

So I looked up the Hittites, and I found out that they were descendants of the Canaanites. There was a curse on the Canaanites, a generation curse that wouldn't stop. So what was

Esau doing? He was bringing that generation curse into his family.

This is why the Bible tells you not to marry a non-Christian, not to be "unequally yoked together" (II Corinthians 6:14). Why? Because they are under the total curse of sin. Do you want your children to be under the curse? Then don't marry an unbeliever. You want your home to be blessed, not cursed; you want your children to be blessed, not cursed.

When you came to Jesus, you began to break that curse. So don't marry an unbeliever and invite a new curse in. That's why Isaac and Rebecca were so upset because they knew that Esau marrying a Canaanite was bringing an unbeliever into their family, allowing the curse into their family.

But God was always concerned to do something to change the family!

That's true. So the next thing we see with this family is the lamb. In Exodus God was very concerned about the family of Israel, and He always had been. He was concerned about Adam and Eve's family, about Seth's family, about Abraham's family. Why? Because not only curses are passed from generation to generation, but also blessings can be too!

Some of your natural talents and strengths are those you've inherited from your parents. And you've probably gotten some spiritual lessons from a grandmother who prayed you in, or a great-grandfather who stood fast when you were a thug or something. Those are blessings that have come down to you.

The Egyptians

And Moses said, Thus saith the LORD, About midnight will I go out into the midst of Egypt: And all the firstborn in the land of Egypt shall die, from the firstborn of Pharaoh that sitteth upon his throne,

*even unto the firstborn of the maidservant that is
behind the mill; and all the firstborn of beasts. And
there shall be a great cry throughout all the land
of Egypt, such as there was none like it, nor shall
be like it any more* (Exodus 11:4-6).

You know how this story goes. The Egyptians had enslaved
the Israelites, and God raised up a Jewish man who was an
adopted son of the Pharaoh to be the deliverer of His true
people from their captors.

Moses warned the Pharaoh again and again, but he kept on
hardening his heart toward God's people, and so the Egyptians
suffered plague after plague: frogs, locusts, polluted water, and
all sorts of infirmities on the land. But Pharaoh continued
rejecting God's warnings, and he and his people continued
under the curse.

Finally, God said, "Now I'm going to judge the Egyptian
family." Notice that He referred to a family unit. "I'm going to
take the firstborn in every Egyptian family." Why? Because the
Egyptian families were under the curse, and "the curse causeless
shall not come."

The Egyptians were wallowing in sin. They worshiped idols
and repented not at all in spite of the dramatic miracles God
brought. God wanted them to repent. He didn't just make the
miracles to get the Israelites out of slavery—He did that too—
but He also wanted to bring the Egyptians into His kingdom.
And some of them did, too.

The Blood of the Lamb

*In the tenth day of this month, they shall take to
them every man a lamb, according to the house of
their fathers, a lamb for an house: . . . and the whole
assembly of the congregation of Israel shall kill it
in the evening. And they shall take of the blood, and*

strike it on the two side posts and on the upper door post of the houses, wherein they shall eat it.

For I will pass through the land of Egypt this night, and will smite all the firstborn in the land of Egypt, both man and beast; and against all the gods of Egypt I will execute judgment: I am the LORD. And the blood shall be to you for a token upon the houses where ye are: and when I see the blood, I will pass over you, and the plague shall not be upon you to destroy you, when I smite the land of Egypt (Exodus 12:3,6,7,12,13).

God said, "So that your family will not be under the curse, you must kill a lamb and put the blood of that lamb over the doorpost of your house." When the Angel of Death passed over, what did he see? He saw the blood of that lamb, and the blood reversed the curse! God said, "The blood will save your family."

What will save your family today? The blood of Jesus. It's not in humanism or psychology. It's not in reading Dr. Spock or "sparing the rod." The blood of Jesus is what will save your family today. The Israelites knew that the blood was the key to their family. The whole key to your family today is the blood of Jesus.

Unequally Yoked

"Yes, but Marilyn, what about when you have married somebody before you were a Christian, then you became a Christian, and they didn't. So what do I have? I have a family curse, and that can't be broken."

That's not true, and I've got one Old Testament and two New Testament scriptures to prove it!

"God setteth the solitary in families: he bringeth out those which are bound with chains: but the rebellious

dwell in a dry land" (Psalms 68:6).

God is saying, "I'll save one in a family, and that will set those free who are bound with chains. I'll take those out who are rebellious, living in a dry land":

> *And the woman which hath an husband that believeth not, and if he be pleased to dwell with her, let her not leave him. For the unbelieving husband is sanctified by the wife, and the unbelieving wife is sanctified by the husband: else were your children unclean: but now are they holy* (I Corinthians 7:13,14).

One believing mate sanctifies the household. And your children are freed from any generation curse:

> *Likewise, ye wives, be in subjection to your own husbands; that, if any obey not the word, they also may without the word be won by the conversation of the wives; While they behold your chaste conversation coupled with fear* (I Peter 3:1,2).

The conversation or the behavior of the wife will be the greatest Christian witness any unbelieving husband will ever see. If it is the husband who is saved, he will love her like Christ loved the Church, and she can't resist the irresistible love of Jesus Christ shown through her husband!

"But it's so hard." Well, Jesus was the first One in our family, and He was solitary too. He was willing to be the only One, and He went to the Cross and was raised from the dead. Why? To bring those of us who were bound with chains and were rebellious in a dry land into the family.

Sometimes it takes just one to break the generation curse. You can be that one! Don't you dare give up and say, "Well, my husband won't come to church—my wife won't come—so I'm going to backslide." If you do that, you are inviting the generation curse back into your family . . . and probably seven times worse!

You certainly don't want the curse on you, or on your husband, or your children, or your grandchildren, or the next generations. The cost of backsliding is too expensive!

Break the Curse . . . Or Be Wiped Out!

God was very concerned that family curses be broken. That's why He absolutely wiped out the Herods. He dealt and dealt with them, but they refused to repent. So after the fourth generation, He wiped them out.

He wiped out the Canaanites. All those "ites" you read about in the Old Testament—the Amorites, the Hittites, the Hivites—are all from the Canaanites. God told Joshua, "When you go in, just wipe out the whole crowd. I dealt with them, and I dealt with them, and they stayed in sin. So I don't want them intermarrying with My people and bringing their generation curses into them." That's why He wiped them out.

The Price That Achan Paid

And Joshua, and all Israel with him, took Achan the son of Zerah, and the silver, and the garment, and the wedge of gold, and his sons, and his daughters, and his oxen, and his asses, and his sheep, and his tent, and all that he had: and they brought them unto the valley of Achor. And Joshua said, Why hast thou troubled us? The LORD shall trouble thee this day. And all Israel stoned him with stones, and burned them with fire, after they had stoned them with stones (Joshua 7:24,25).

Achan was from the tribe of Judah. Originally he was a believer, but he stole a Babylonian garment and some gold and silver. God said, "I gave you a chance to repent, to sanctify the people." But Achan didn't repent. So finally the Holy Spirit pointed him out as the guilty one.

The Israelites didn't just stone Achan—they also stoned his wife and his children. Why? Because God said, "I don't want that curse going on in My people. I don't want the next generation to be thieves, and the generation after. They won't repent, so wipe them out." So Achan paid the heavy price that a backslider pays.

What happens when you become a believer? We need to know how to deal with this because I believe a lot of the problems Wally and I encountered with our adopted son Michael were because we didn't know about generation curses.

Many of the problems with your natural-born children are generation curses. When you check it out, some of the problems we deal with in ourselves—insecurity, fear, poverty, high-level anger, violence—are the way that your father acted, or your mother, or your grandmother, or your grandfather. But you tell the devil that he isn't going to do that to your house!

You say, "This house has been cleansed. The blood of Jesus is over it, and you're not bringing seven other evil spirits in. This is not your house; this is my house, and it belongs to Jesus! Satan, you stop this in the name of Jesus! This house will never be yours! It will never be yours in my children or in my children's children."

A pastor told about this happening in his family. He said that his daughter started to get into some sin. He took his Bible and read to her the part about the curses, and then said, "Now this is what happens when you get into these things. Is that what you want for your life?" She answered, "No!"

He said, "Well, that's what is happening. These curses have come down on you, and now is the time for them to stop. Do you want to stop them?" And she wanted to stop them.

We need to show our children the truth: "Hey, if you curse me, and you act rebelliously toward me, you're putting a curse on yourself"; or, "If you get into sexual sins, you're putting a curse on yourself."

If you were in that yucky sin yourself, you might as well level with your kids and say, "I blew it when I was your age, but I don't want this thing coming on you. I had a weakness in this area, but I've repented, and God cleansed me. And you're not going to get it in you."

Everyday Curses

There are some basic curses in the Bible which deal with the way we live today, in this century.

Don't put your trust in some man and depart from the Lord:

"Thus saith the LORD, Cursed be the man that trusteth in man, and maketh flesh his arm, and whose heart departeth from the LORD" (Jeremiah 17:5).

We see this happening in our political system. Some good-looking guy gets up and runs for governor or senator or congressman, and we get all excited: "Oh, this fellow is going to make some big changes in our country! He's smart, he's compassionate, he's experienced, he's got the big picture!" Then he blows it in some area—maybe it's big, maybe it's little—and we wonder, "What happened to him?"

That man needs to be relying not on his own good looks, or his charisma, or his smarts . . . but every day of his private and public life, he needs to be on his knees before God asking for divine wisdom and guidance! We shouldn't put our trust in him, and he shouldn't be trusting anyone but God the Father. When we put our trust in a man, we're bringing a curse upon our nation.

We see people get married, and they do a drop-out with God.

"Hey! You wanted a husband so badly. Now you've got one, and you give up the Lord." You're putting your trust in a man, and you're bringing a curse on your marriage. Do you want your marriage to be blessed? Then put God at the center of it.

You can't trust in your work:

> *"Cursed be he that doeth the work of the LORD deceitfully, and cursed be he that keepeth back his sword from blood"* (Jeremiah 48:10).

If you do God's work in a deceitful way, you can bring a curse. That's all too obvious with the "televangelist" scandals that have rocked our nation:

> *"And whatsoever ye do, do it heartily, as to the Lord, and not unto men"* (Colossians 3:23).

Every kind of job there is, keep in mind that your true Master is not your supervisor or your boss, but your Lord.

If you put your trust in your work, you've got a curse on your situation. Your trust has to be in the blood. Your source is not your paycheck—your source is Jesus Christ.

You can't steal from God and trust in your own money. "Well, I can't afford to tithe." Do you know what you're really saying? "I trust my money more than I trust God's Word." That will bring a curse:

> *"Ye are cursed with a curse: for ye have robbed me, . . . "* (Malachi 3:9).

You refuse to tithe, and you personally bring the curse into your life.

Chapter Eight
REVERSING THE CURSE

Blessings Started With Abraham

"And I will bless them that bless thee; and curse him that curseth thee: . . . " (Genesis 12:3).

Now here is what God said: "I want to turn the curse into a blessing. I want the thing that has cursed you to come around and bless you." There is a place where God reversed the curse for families.

Now how did Abraham get in on this thing anyway? By faith. When we come to Jesus and we take His blood, we have to take it by . . . faith. We take His Word by faith. When we use our faith, what begins to happen? The thing that cursed us back there is now going to turn around and bless us!

When people come against us, hating us, God said, "Those that bless you, I will bless; but those that curse you, I will curse. I will reverse this thing; it won't work against you, it will work for you."

When the enemy comes against us to curse us, he ends up getting hurt, and we end up getting blessed! Why? Because we are Abraham's seed, and we are walking by faith.

Even when we blow it, and we repent of it, the devil would still like to pull a number on us. When Balaam went to curse the Israelites—and he was ready to curse them thoroughly— he couldn't curse them. The king of Moab got so mad at him and said, "Why don't you curse these people? I told you to curse them, and you keep blessing them!"

Balaam answered, "You just can't curse what God has blessed." That's the truth! The Word says that you can't curse what God has blessed, and that's our family blessing!

> *"How shall I curse, whom God hath not cursed? or how shall I defy, whom the LORD hath not defied?"* (Numbers 23:8).

Here's what you claim: "We've got God's blessing in our new family. The old family may have had a lot of curses!"

My Own Story

My father had two serious nervous breakdowns. When I met Wally, my dad was in the midst of a nervous breakdown, and I was afraid that he couldn't give me away in our wedding. It was so bad, he had shock treatments and the whole thing. And my mother had a nervous breakdown when I was eight years old.

So you can imagine the number the devil wanted to do on me! I didn't understand generation curses then, and I didn't always understand what was the devil's voice. But the light of God and the revelation knowledge of His Word is greater today than it ever was before. It is gaining ascendancy in people's lives and hearts. We live in a wonderful day of the revelation of God's Word and knowing how to overcome the enemy and live victoriously.

The devil said to me, "You're going to have a nervous breakdown because you are so like your father. You look like him, you act like him, you think like him." And that's all true. I really do look like my father, and I take after him in many ways. So the enemy said, "You're going to have a nervous breakdown."

This was when I was thirty-six years old. The devil was lying to me, and I was thinking, "Oh, I have so much pressure!" I didn't even know what pressure was then. I was living in a country club compared to the work I do now!

A lot of this is an attitude of thought. If we get our thinking right with God, nothing is impossible. We can do all kinds of things. We can shake nations!

So I heard the voice of the devil, and I went down into the basement of our house. He said, "Kill yourself. You don't want to have a nervous breakdown and embarrass your husband. He's a pastor, and they'll say, 'That poor man. His wife had a nervous breakdown. She's an idiot in some place scratching the walls.' What an embarrassment to Wally. Just kill yourself, and then you won't embarrass him."

This attack from the devil was so heavy that I cried out, "God, help me! I'm just like my father, and I'm going to have a nervous breakdown!"

He answered, "That's right. You're just like your Father. I'm your Father, and I've never had a nervous breakdown, and you never will either." And that was the end of it.

That stupid devil! What he intended for a curse became a blessing, because you cannot curse what God has blessed!

Stay out of sin, stay in the Word, and you can't walk in a curse. All you can do is get blessed. When the world tries to curse you, the more He'll bless you if you stay in the Word. But if you get into sin, you bring a curse.

The Battle Is in the Mind

When we deal with our children, we need to teach them about curses and blessings. We need to show them how to come against those things themselves.

The light of God's Word needs to be in their minds:

> *In whom the god of this world hath blinded the minds of them which believe not, lest the light of the glorious gospel of Christ, who is the image of God, should shine unto them* (II Corinthians 4:4).

The devil's real toe hold is in the mind. If we can capture our children's minds with the Word—saturating and cleansing their minds (and ours) with the Word—then the enemy can't get a toe hold:

> *"And they overcame him by the blood of the Lamb, and by the word of their testimony; . . . "* (Revelation 12:11).

We overcome the enemy by the blood of the Lamb—and since you're a born-again believer, this means the blood is available to you—and by the Word of our testimony—which is using God's Word as a weapon against the enemy. We give our children the Word, and they quote the Word back to the devil . . . and he can't stand it, and he leaves!

Our children then decide: "This is a generation curse. But I don't have to be under it. I am going to come under the generation blessing of God!"

The Boomerang Effect

> *And seeing a fig tree afar off having leaves, he came, if haply he might find any thing thereon: and when he came to it, he found nothing but leaves; for the time of figs was not yet. And Jesus answered and said unto it, No man eat fruit of thee hereafter for ever. And his disciples heard it. And in the morning, as they passed by, they saw the fig tree dried up from the roots. And Peter calling to remembrance saith unto him, Master, behold, the fig tree which thou cursedst is withered away. And Jesus answering saith unto them, Have faith in God. For verily I*

72

say unto you, That whosoever shall say unto this mountain, Be thou removed, and be thou cast into the sea; and shall not doubt in his heart, but shall believe that those things which he saith shall come to pass; he shall have whatsoever he saith (Mark 11:13,14,20-23).

What did Jesus mean here? He had cursed the fig tree because it didn't have any fruit. When He and the disciples came back, and they discovered that it had really worked, He said to them, "You can do the same thing."

We don't take the curse, we give the curse! And to whom do we give the curse? The devil. We curse him and his works with the name of Jesus! We curse what he is trying to do to our nation. We curse incest. We curse pornography.

The devil can't bring a curse on us because we have the blood of Jesus and His righteousness that have cleansed us from our sin. We have the Word against him. We are the ones who are in authority to curse his work. The roles are reversed. We need to take our role and curse the circumstances.

We talked about politics before. When you vote, I trust you are praying about the right person to vote for and that you're cursing the work of the devil who tries to put in the wrong person.

Your responsibility is to pray and to vote. We shouldn't lie down and play dead, saying, "Well, I'm a Christian. I just read my Bible. I don't vote." You need to read your Bible and pray and vote. You need to be active, and you need to curse the work that the devil is doing.

People Problems

"Okay, Marilyn, but what do I do about people? There are those who come against me, who hurt me and wound me. What do I do about them?" Well, you must understand that the devil will send anybody along to give you a hassle:

> *But I say unto you, Love your enemies, bless them that curse you, do good to them that hate you, and pray for them that despitefully use you, and persecute you* (Matthew 5:44).

You want to reverse the curse of people's opinion. They may dislike you, they may gossip about you, they may say ugly things about you . . . but what did God tell you to do to them? You must reverse their curse, turning their curses into blessings. How? You bless them, you pray for them, you do good to them, you love them.

What happens? *"When a man's ways please the LORD, he maketh even his enemies to be at peace with him"* (Proverbs 16:7). The people who were against you will either shut up, or they'll be for you . . . if you do it God's way! This is the way we reverse the curse.

God didn't put us here just to break the family curse—although that certainly is a biggie!—but He also put us here to break the curse on the earth of what the enemy is trying to do. He put us here to break the curse of strife and confusion.

Don't be a part of bringing strife. Don't be ugly and nasty. Don't be a backbiter and a gossip. You shut your mouth, or you'll bring a curse on yourself.

When you have people coming against you, you reverse the curse by saying, "Let's see . . . what nice thing could I do for them? I could have them to dinner . . . . " But don't poison them! Do something really nice—be sweet to them.

What's that called?

> *Therefore if thine enemy hunger, feed him; if he thirst, give him drink: for in so doing thou shalt heap coals*

of fire on his head. Be not overcome of evil, but
overcome evil with good (Romans 12:20,21).

You protest, "But I would have to just swallow everything to
do that!" Job said:

"Neither have I suffered my mouth to sin by wishing
a curse to his soul" (Job 31:30).

Did you ever wish something bad would happen to somebody
who's been bad to you? Have you ever thought, "I wonder how
old they are? Maybe they'll die pretty soon, and that will end
it." Or did you ever wish they'd just move to another city? Or,
"I wish something bad would happen in their family, and then
they'd learn what this is all about."

Years ago, there was a woman in our church who had four
children. She always told us how perfect her children were and
how bad everybody else's kids were. When she'd be going on
and on about her kids, I used to think, "I hope something bad
happens to her."

But then the Lord dealt with me: "Stop that! You're going
to bring something on yourself." I repented of that!

If you say with your mouth that you want something bad to
happen to them, you're wishing a curse to your soul. You are
sinning. Don't wish for something bad; pray for something good.
The goodness of God leads them to repentance. That's the way
you reverse the curse!

Chapter Nine
RESPONDING TO GOD

"Well, Marilyn, I had a difficult time coming up with some family curses. Frankly, I don't like the idea of looking under every bush for devils and curses. But I did it like you asked me to, although I really didn't have any real biggies to break." I have an answer for that.

Sometimes in some areas of our lives, we think, "Why is that not working? What is wrong?" We raise children to serve the Lord, and then—bang!—they go haywire at a certain age. Then we ask, "What is this? God, I've got to have some answers!"

" . . . *he that is spiritual judgeth* [understands] *all things, . . .* " (I Corinthians 2:15); or " . . . *they that seek the* LORD *understand all things"* (Proverbs 28:5).

Many times we have to wait on the Lord, and He gives us the answer. Another translation says, *"He that is in the Spirit understands all things."*

As you wait on God, as you are in the Spirit, then He opens your understanding to see what the problem is and how to get rid of it. God never just identifies a problem and then leaves you to deal with it alone. He always gives you the solution to the problem and often the miracle that can turn it around.

So the Bible says that some negative hereditary things are curses. Curses always start with sin, for " . . . *the curse causeless shall not come"* (Proverbs 26:2). Sin takes a number of forms:

worshiping other gods (such as money or career) . . . a lust for power . . . rebellious children . . . cruelty . . . violence . . . sexual sins:

> " . . . *he that committeth fornication sinneth against his own body*" (I Corinthians 6:18).

Sexual sin is one of the worst kinds of curses because of what it does to the person. Adultery not only hurts you physically, but it leaves scar tissue on your soul. Then your children have the same weakness, and then your grandchildren and your great-grandchildren.

Breaking the Curse of Hereditary Disease

Another curse that gets passed from generation to generation is disease. I recall several years ago teaching at a Bible study in a home in Denver, and a Baptist attended the Bible study where we were studying healing.

During the Bible study she just wouldn't sit down, and it bothered me. I thought she was antagonistic toward the Bible study. Afterward I talked with her, and she said, "Well, you may say that healing is for today, but I don't believe it." Then she told me about two very desperate needs she had.

Her father was blind. He had a hereditary eye disease that would usually hit his family in their early thirties. Their eyes would gradually get worse and worse until—by the time they were in their forties—they were completely blind.

This woman was in her middle thirties, and she was starting to go blind. But even worse than that, her teenage daughter was beginning to go blind too. What did we have here? We had a generation curse!

I didn't know about generation curses at that time, but the more knowledge we get, the more we know how to attack the enemy and set people free:

"My people are destroyed [perish] *for lack of knowledge: . . . "* (Hosea 4:6).

The more of the Word that we get, the less we're going to perish.

This woman was literally perishing, and so was her daughter. She didn't believe what we were studying, but she needed that healing badly. And not only was she losing her sight, but I discovered that the reason she had been standing all during the Bible study was that her hip bone had been operated on, and part of the bone had been removed. She couldn't sit comfortably for a very long period of time. She needed healing badly!

A well-known evangelist was coming to town, and some of the people in the Bible study invited her to go with them to his meetings, but she refused. Then her daughter said, "Mother, it can't hurt to go one time." So she and her daughter went.

They were sitting in the balcony of the auditorium, and the evangelist called out for people who had problems in their hips or in their bone structure. The daughter said, "Mother, stand up! It won't hurt."

It certainly didn't hurt. She felt the warmth of the Lord go all over her. She knew something had happened, but she didn't know how to identify it.

That night as she was getting ready for bed, her daughter came in the bedroom and was talking with her. Then the daughter said, "Mother, there's an extra lump on you." The bone had been removed, so nothing showed. The daughter said, "Mother, feel for yourself. I think you have a hip bone now!"

The mother felt her hip, and she had a new hip bone! God had done a miracle! Her spirit caught on fire after that!

She came back to the Bible study and said, "I believe in

healing! I believe in healing!" She told us her story, then she said, "Now I want to pray for my eyes."

We rebuked the devil and prayed for her eyes . . . and she has 20/20 vision today! And her daughter who was going blind is not blind today because the generation curse was broken!

Setting Our Generations Free

Deuteronomy 28:46 is an unusual verse:

"And they shall be upon thee for a sign and for a wonder, and upon thy seed for ever."

I love to study signs and wonders in the New Testament, outside of the devil's lying signs and wonders. But this scripture refers to bad types of signs and wonders. It says that these curses which come from generation to generation will be signs and wonders of the demonic power of sin and the power of the devil to keep something going on throughout a family's history.

Now we know the way for things to get better! We have been bound for years by a lot of junk and trash of the devil, but now not only can we be set free, but also we can set our generations free! We can overcome those nasty familiar spirits and set ourselves free and our children free and our children's children free "to a thousand generations" (Deuteronomy 7:9):

But if I cast out devils by the Spirit of God, then the kingdom of God is come unto you. Or else how can one enter into a strong man's house, and spoil his goods, except he first bind the strong man? And then he will spoil his house (Matthew 12:28,29).

We know that we can spoil the devil's stronghold in our households by binding him in the name of Jesus, by telling him that he can't do those awful things to our house or to our generation or to the generations that follow us.

Those evil spirits that are familiar with your family for generations know that you are already born with a weakness. When it's time, they make their attack on you. But you bind him, and you're not going to be a diabetic! You bind him, and you're not going to get into sexual sin! You bind him, and you're not going to live in poverty!

But remember: once you are cleansed, he's going to come back and try to take your children. If he gets them, he's going to make them seven times worse! But we don't have to let it happen to our children: we can set them free too! We don't have to put up with it any more.

Releasing Bitterness

Did you know that God wants you to be free? Did you know that the Word is always freeing?

> "... *where the Spirit of the Lord is, there is liberty*" (II Corinthians 3:17).

God wants to make you free in every area of your life. He wants you to go kick the devil in the teeth:

> *"Looking diligently lest any man fail of the grace of God; lest any root of bitterness springing up trouble you, and thereby many be defiled"* (Hebrews 12:15).

With all that we've learned, it's pretty easy for us to read this verse and say, "Yes, that's right. Bitterness is definitely a cause of family curses. People who are bitter because of something bad that happened to their father or their great-grandfather are probably not going to get very far with family blessings. They've got to get rid of that bitterness."

Well, that's very true. But the cure for bitterness is forgiveness, and that's one attribute most humans have a problem with: true, deep-from-the-heart, long-lasting forgiveness—the kind that also forgets:

81

"I, even I, am he that blotteth out thy transgressions for mine own sake, and will not remember thy sins" (Isaiah 43:25).

Whereby are given unto us exceeding great and precious promises: that by these ye might be partakers of the divine nature, having escaped the corruption that is in the world through lust (II Peter 1:4).

True forgiveness is a divine attribute. But we now have the nature of God in us, and that makes us partakers of all His divine attributes, including genuine forgiveness and everlasting ability not to become bitter.

Esau Again

"And the boys grew: and Esau was a cunning hunter, a man of the field; and Jacob was a plain man, dwelling in tents" (Genesis 25:27).

Looking diligently lest any man fail of the grace of God; lest any root of bitterness springing up trouble you, and thereby many be defiled; Lest there be any fornicator, or profane person, as Esau, who for one morsel of meat sold his birthright. For ye know how that afterward, when he would have inherited the blessing, he was rejected: for he found no place of repentance, though he sought it carefully with tears (Hebrews 12:15-17).

There is more that we can learn from the life of Esau. He was a profane man. I thought, "What's profane? Does that mean he used profanity, that he cursed a lot?"

The Bible says that "Esau was a cunning hunter, a man of the field." That sort of pictures Esau as being a "macho man"— one of those guys who likes to hunt, fish, and wrestle with the boys. "Jacob was a plain man, dwelling in tents." Jacob sounds like a mild-mannered type, engaging in intellectual conversation with the ladies of the camp. The two brothers—who were twins—couldn't have been more different!

But here *profane* doesn't necessarily refer to Esau's language. It means that he was worldly, that he was very earth conscious. He was an earthy person. When he woke up in the morning, he thought, "What's for breakfast? What am I going to eat all day?"

His whole thing was his physical body. He was proud of his hairy chest and his strong arms to pull a bow. He was proud of his ability to run fast and wrestle everything down. His physical prowess made his father proud of him too. But Rebekah favored the gentle Jacob.

However, Esau's preoccupation with his physique and with his ego led him to be a fornicator. Fornication can either be sexual sin, or there can be spiritual fornication. Esau went after idols—his own ego included—rather than after the living God. He treated spiritual things very lightly.

One day he came in from a hard day of hunting and horseback riding and other "macho man" activities, and he was hungry. And there was his brother Jacob stirring a little pot of stew.

Now remember that Esau was always thinking of his stomach, always thinking of his physical comforts. He said to Jacob, "I would like what you're cooking."

And Jacob answered, "Well, I would like your birthright, so we'll just swap." Frankly, that wasn't very nice of Jacob to suggest such a thing, to respond to Esau's insignificant moment of hunger by countering with one of the powerful things of God.

That goes to show that the devil is always on the prowl, "... *seeking whom he may devour*" (I Peter 5:8), just watching for us to mistreat the holy things of God in a moment of jesting or lightheartedness, because then he can pervert God's plan for our lives. We have to be on guard, to bring "... *into captivity every thought to the obedience of Christ*" (II Corinthians 10:5); and "... *whatsoever ye do in word or deed, do all in the name of the Lord Jesus, ...*" (Colossians 3:17). Because when Jacob answered Esau with "I want your birthright," he was contributing to this change in the course of history forever!

And so Esau sold his birthright for a piece of meat. After he did that—after he ate all the stew and was lying around with a comfortably full belly—then he felt bad about it. But he didn't repent to God. He didn't say, "Dear God, You've given me so much! How could I have treated the gift that You gave me so lightly?" He just felt sorry that he had missed out on a bargain.

We can be sorry that we get caught in sin, but we're not sorry that we sinned and hurt God, or even hurt other people. We're just sorry for the backslam that we got. That is not godly repentance. It does not bring forth the faithful or beautiful fruits of righteousness.

The Curse of Depression

Do you know what most depression is? Earthly sorrow. You are in sin when you're depressed.

People want to be petted when they're depressed. "Oh, be nice to me, treat me sweetly because I'm depressed." They are really on one of those "Woe is me! Pity me!" kicks. But the Lord is not going to sympathize with you because depression is unbelief, and unbelief is a sin!

Often depression is unconfessed sin. You didn't deal with it yourself, thinking somebody else has treated you wrongly. But depression is giving in to sin, and that's a curse. It can lead to mental and emotional breakdown. It can lead to serious psychotic disorders. It can lead to insanity. And it can be passed from one generation to the next.

So Esau lost his birthright, and he also lost his blessing. Jacob just sailed in and grabbed the blessing. Jacob was wrong in the way he did it, and so was Rebekah. But their opportunity was created because of Esau's sin.

Esau lost his birthright, and he lost his blessing, so he ran into Isaac's tent and cried. He said, "Oh Daddy, I've lost my birthright!" Whose fault was it? It was Esau's own fault, but he didn't say that. "Oh Daddy, I've lost my blessing! Please, please! I feel so sorry about this!" This is earthly sorrow. "Please, don't you have another blessing?"

He sought a place of repentance because he was trying to get his father to relent and give him a blessing. But he never got it. He got just a little of the leftover blessing. "He sought it with tears," but he never got it.

Esau did not use godly sorrow, he used earthly sorrow. If he had used godly sorrow, he would have said, "God, how I failed, and how I blew it!" Instead he said, "God, how Jacob failed, and how he blew it! And look at my mother; she's not even for me! They failed me!"

Esau became bitter in his heart against his brother and against his mother—although the Word says, *"Honour thy father and thy mother, . . . "* (Deuteronomy 5:16)—and probably a little against God too. Esau never used the godly repentance which would have cleansed him and set him free. He became defiled by his bitterness when he could have reversed the curse by repenting of his part in it.

That's the difference. We want everybody else to repent, but we think we don't need to because we're so sweet. "Why should I have to repent? I didn't do anything that bad."

Esau sold the birthright, so he obviously didn't think that the blessing was too important. Later he wanted to murder Jacob for what he had done. "It's Jacob's fault! It's Mama's fault!" He was so wrapped up in his self-pity that he never realized that godly repentance would remove his fault, would change the situation!

As long as you cop out, you will experience depression, and you will experience bitterness. When you are bitter, you defile yourself . . . and you may defile others too. Esau defiled his generations, which is a tragedy.

Bitter Fathers—Bitter Children

Bitterness is a luxury you cannot afford. It's too expensive. It will defile you, and it will defile those around you:

> " . . . *The fathers have eaten a sour grape, and the children's teeth are set on edge*" (Jeremiah 31:29).

That's exactly what happened to Esau. When Esau became bitter against Jacob and Jacob's descendants, his children became bitter against Jacob's descendants too:

> *And Moses sent messengers from Kadesh unto the king of Edom, Thus saith thy brother Israel, Thou knowest all the travail that hath befallen us: How our fathers went down into Egypt, and we have dwelt in Egypt a long time; and the Egyptians vexed us, and our fathers: And when we cried unto the LORD, he heard our voice, and sent an angel, and hath brought us forth out of Egypt: and, behold, we are in Kadesh, a city in the uttermost of thy border: Let us pass, I pray thee, through thy country: we will not pass through the fields, or through the vineyards, neither will we drink of the water of the wells: we will go by the king's high way, we will not turn to the right hand nor to the left, until we*

have passed thy borders.

And Edom said unto him, Thou shalt not pass by me, lest I come out against thee with the sword. And the children of Israel said unto him, We will go by the high way: and if I and my cattle drink of thy water, then I will pay for it: I will only, without doing any thing else, go through on my feet. And he said, Thou shalt not go through. And Edom came out against him with much people, and with a strong hand. Thus Edom refused to give Israel passage through his border: wherefore Israel turned away from him (Numbers 20:14-21).

Edom was the country that belonged to Esau and his descendants. When the Israelites came out of Egypt, they said, "We need to pass through Edom on our way to the Promised Land. If you will let us pass through, we will pay for the water that our animals drink and that we drink. We will pay for the grass that they eat. We will pay for everything."

But the Edomites said, "No! We hate the descendants of Jacob. You can't come through here." What did the descendants of Jacob ever do to the Edomites? Nothing!

This is over 400 years after Jacob got Esau's blessing! What did the Israelites do to the Edomites? Nothing! But the Edomites were bitter. Their "teeth were set on edge" because of Esau's bitterness against Jacob.

You may be bitter against someone. It may go back into your childhood, when some teacher yelled at you in school—or when the factory closed down and your father lost his job, and you had to get an after-school job to contribute to the family's income. Maybe your husband is all wrapped up in his job, and you're becoming bitter because it looks like he cares more about his work than he does about you.

If you are bitter against someone, you can't afford it! It's going to cost you your blessing. And it can cost your children's blessing too. You had better repent. You are wrong to be bitter, and you're going to live in depression and defeat until you repent of it. Bitterness is dangerous!

This bitterness followed Esau all the way down through his descendants. Saul had a problem with Esau's descendants. David had a problem with the Edomites. Practically every king of Judah and some of the kings of the northern kingdom had trouble with Esau's seed. They were always bugging Jacob's descendants and giving them a hard time. Why? Because their father ate sour grapes, and all the generations' teeth are set on edge.

Then in the New Testament, we have the Idumeans. The Idumeans were descendants of the Edomites. The four Herods were Idumean, which meant they were Edomites too.

Did they say, "Oh, here comes Jesus! We just love Jesus. We want to serve Jesus!" They never said that. Herod the Great said, "Where is He? I want to worship Him" (Matthew 2:8) . . . but he didn't want to worship Jesus, he wanted to kill Him!

So Herod had all the male babies under two years of age murdered. Why? Because there was a bitterness toward any of God's seed. It started with Esau, and hundreds of years later Herod's teeth were still being set on edge.

"But Marilyn, that's so terrible!" That's right. But Herod could have repented. He had heard the Word from the wise men, and he knew of the miraculous star. The instant he would have repented, that generation curse could have been broken!

The instant you repent of your sins, the curse is broken. But as long as you cop out, as long as you dump the blame on everybody else and what you think they've done to you, then the curse will NOT be broken in your life.

You will continue to be depressed. You will continue to be bitter. And you will sow sourness in the lives of others. It's not worth it. You just can't afford it!

Each of the four Herods in the Bible had his chance to repent and break that longstanding curse. Each one of them heard God's Word—and a couple of them were "almost persuaded"— but they ended up turning their backs on God instead. And they turned around and committed some horrible crimes— including murdering one or two or several hundred babies— thus fulfilling their part of the family curse.

After four generations of trying to save the Herod family from their cursed Canaanite heritage, God said, "Enough." And the last Herod died. There are no more Herods around today either!

If you are "almost persuaded" to repent of your sins, then your "almost" is not enough, and you will be a failure. You stand to lose everything—your entire family may die out!—if you don't stop those generation curses right now.

You must say, "I repent of everything. I'm not going to hold bitterness in my heart." And then when you repent, you are free, and the generation curse is broken. You can free the next generation so that something seven times worse won't come upon them. Don't be like Esau who ate sour grapes and defiled all of his generations.

Chapter Ten
JOB AND HIS HOUSEHOLD

And the LORD said unto Satan, Hast thou considered my servant Job, that there is none like him in the earth, a perfect and an upright man, one that feareth God, and escheweth evil? Then Satan answered the LORD, and said, Doth Job fear God for nought? Hast not thou made an hedge about him, and about his house, and about all that he hath on every side? thou hast blessed the work of his hands, and his substance is increased in the land. But put forth thine hand now, and touch all that he hath, and he will curse thee to thy face. And the LORD said unto Satan, Behold, all that he hath is in thy power; only upon himself put not forth thine hand. In all this Job sinned not, nor charged God foolishly (Job 1:8-12,22).

Job was another man who suffered from bitterness. All the awful things that happened to him were not entirely his fault, for God allowed the calamities to come upon him as a test of his heart and as proof to the devil.

At first Job didn't blame God for his troubles:

"In all this Job sinned not, nor charged God foolishly" (Job 1:22).

But as his "friends"—Eliphaz the Temanite, Bildad the Shuhite, and Zophar the Naamathite—continued to erode his confidence in God, he developed a bitterness of heart.

That's why it's so important for you to associate with positive-talking people and not let yourself be pulled down to the level of those who love to wallow in gloom and doom.

Job started to complain. Complaining and bitterness are like Siamese twins: you can't separate them. Complaining is a very dangerous thing because you are really saying, "I don't believe God can do anything about this. I don't believe people can change." If you are in bitterness, if you start to complain, then you are in trouble, and you need to shut up.

To be honest, if I had been Job, and I had gone through all the things he did, I probably would have been bitter too. He'd lost his children; he'd lost his wealth; he'd lost his health. He also had three wretched friends.

So Job had these things happen to him, and he said, *"I will complain in the bitterness of my soul"* (Job 7:11).

Here is where we get into trouble. We say, "I have a right to be bitter." No you don't; bitterness is simply too expensive!

It goes on:

"I will speak in the bitterness of my soul" (Job 10:1).

He said, "I'm so bitter. Things are so hard. It wasn't my fault. Why did this happen? Things are so bad."

"Ye Shall Know the Truth . . . "

When we look at Job's situation, we say, "Poor Job, he had it so hard." But we don't need sympathy when we have it hard. We need the Word to set us free! Sympathy and pity put us in a place that allows the thing to keep on defiling us. But the Word sets us free:

Now no chastening for the present seemeth to be

joyous, but grievous: nevertheless afterward it yieldeth the peaceable fruit of righteousness unto them which are exercised thereby (Hebrews 12:11).

If you practice godly sorrow, you'll get the "peaceable fruit of righteousness." But if you get into earthly sorrow, you're going to be depressed forever. And depression and bitterness are all in the same package.

The Curse of Fear

What's the other feeling that happened to Job? Fear:

"For the thing which I greatly feared is come upon me, and that which I was afraid of is come unto me" (Job 3:25).

"Fear came upon me, and trembling, which made all my bones to shake" (Job 4:14).

It looks like Job's weakness was already known to the devil because he was able to exploit that weakness so thoroughly. Job's own fearfulness contributed to the virulence of the curse that the devil brought on him.

Your fear can contribute to a curse entering into your life:

"There is no fear in love; but perfect love casteth out fear: because fear hath torment. He that feareth is not made perfect in love" (I John 4:18).

Fear is one of the devil's favorite tools because it is so subtle. A little worry can grow into a medium-sized concern, which grows into a huge mountain of fear. When you are weighed down with a mountain of fear, then you won't be much good in spiritual warfare!

I remember a lady who married late in life and had two children. She was a real fussbudget about her kids. Any time one of them would sneeze once or twice, she had the thermometer out and was stuffing him into a sweater. The first sign of a little rash or puffy eyes, and she was wringing her hands and saying, "Oh dear! My little one has a terrible allergy!"

That little child heard his mommy talking that way, and he began to be very picky about what he would eat. "Oh, I can't eat that because Mommy says I'm allergic to that kind of food." Within a short time that little child developed full-blown allergies to certain foods, and those allergies threatened his life!

I believe that woman worried and fussed and feared those very allergies into her child's life. She walked in doubt and fearfulness, rather than in confidence in God's Word, and her fear allowed the devil to launch a sneak attack on her family. Her fear was a sin, and sins always bring a curse.

" . . . And the Truth Will Set You Free!"

So these three men ceased to answer Job, because he was righteous in his own eyes. Then was kindled the wrath of Elihu the son of Barachel the Buzite, of the kindred of Ram: against Job was his wrath kindled, because he justified himself rather than God (Job 32:1,2).

Now God got to Job. With all this stuff happening to him, Job was murmuring and complaining and protesting to God that he was so righteous. He was full of self-righteousness! He said, "Paint me white because I'm so good."

His three friends—Eliphaz, Bildad, and Zophar—even got fed up with his nonstop complaining and his stuffy self-righteousness, and they left him. So God used another young man, Elihu, to speak on His behalf; He gave Elihu the Word of God to bring to Job:

But there is a spirit in man: and the inspiration of the Almighty giveth them understanding. For I am

full of matter, the spirit within me constraineth me
(Job 32:8,18).

God—speaking through Elihu—said, "Job, you think you're white because you're so full of your self-righteousness, but I'm painting you black because you're so bad. You're bitter; you're complaining; you're into depression; you're into self-pity. But you don't even know what's going on here!"

If we get in the Spirit, we will understand things—*"the inspiration of the Almighty giveth them understanding"* (Job 32:8)—and we'll know how to get the situation set free. As long as we try to handle it in the flesh, we don't get the spiritual revelation of it:

> *Then the LORD answered Job out of the whirlwind, and said, Who is this that darkeneth counsel by words without knowledge? Gird up now thy loins like a man; for I will demand of thee, and answer thou me. Where wast thou when I laid the foundations of the earth? declare, if thou hast understanding* (Job 38:1-4).

Then God Himself came to Job and said, "Who do you think you are anyway? You don't even know one thing about this situation."

Job recognized the voice of God. He didn't get all puffed up and say, "Well, if that's the way God is going to talk to me, I'm going to change churches!" When Job stopped talking about himself long enough to listen, he heard God speaking:

> *"Wherefore I abhor myself, and repent in dust and ashes"* (Job 42:6).

Job didn't say, "I abhor my wife. She's got the longest tongue. Why did I ever get stuck with her?" Or he didn't say, "I abhor my friends. Have you been listening to what they're saying? God,

I'm so disgusted. I hope You kick them really hard. I hope You really get them because they came to comfort me, and instead they made me feel worse. So go get them, God!"

No, what Job did say was, "I abhor myself." Does that sound like genuine godly repentance to you? Who do we have to repent for? If you don't know how to answer that, then you need to ask the Holy Spirit to show it to you.

"Marilyn, you're really stepping on my toes!" Well, this stepped on my own toes too because it made me realize that I still had some bitterness in my heart.

Remember my great-grandfather who was cruel? The curse came down through our family, and that same cruelty was trying to come into me. We were under a generation curse! When I realized that—when I saw that I had bitterness in my heart against my father and my brother—then I repented of that bitterness, and I repented of the cruelty . . . and the curse was broken!

I don't take after that side of the family—I take after the Jesus side! I've got a new Father, and He's got a new nature, and I broke that curse . . . and my daughter Sarah is never going to take that thing either!

So, like Job, I said, "I abhor myself. I repent in ashes. God, I'm the one who is wrong. It's not my father's fault. It's not my mother's fault. I am wrong. Forgive me. I have sinned and hurt You, and I have sinned and hurt others."

The Blood Reverses the Curse

Therefore take unto you now seven bullocks and seven rams, and go to my servant Job, and offer up for yourselves a burnt offering; and my servant Job shall pray for you: . . . (Job 42:8).

When Job repented, watch what God did. He said, "Offer

a sacrifice"—because it's through the blood that the curse is reversed—"and pray for your friends."

"Pray for them? I don't want to pray for my friends. Let's burn them for the sacrifice!" No, that's not what Job said. He was repentant and obedient to the Lord. He responded to God's Word. So what happened? Watch:

"And the LORD turned the captivity of Job, when he prayed for his friends: also the LORD gave Job twice as much as he had before" (Job 42:10).

When Job prayed for his friends, his captivity was turned. Do you want your captivity to be turned? Do you want to reverse the curse in your life?

But I say unto you, Love your enemies, bless them that curse you, do good to them that hate you, and pray for them which despitefully use you, and persecute you (Matthew 5:44).

If you want your captivity turned, then you'd better bless those who have persecuted you and have spoken against you. You'd better forgive them, and ask God to forgive you for your part in it because nobody is totally lily white.

When you do that, just watch God turn your captivity! He will turn it around because you have reversed the generation curse. And when you do that, something happens with your seed and with the seed that is to come.

Teach your children: "Don't you get into this. If the devil comes to tempt you with this, you tell him, 'Get out of here! I'm not under the generation curse. I'm under the blessings of a new heavenly Father, and I have a new nature.'"

Chapter Eleven

GOOD FROM EVIL

We've studied all sorts of families in this book. We've studied the family of Abraham and the Herod family. We've learned about blessed families, and we've learned about cursed families. Now we're going to look at a couple more families.

The House of Omri

"In the thirty and first year of Asa king of Judah began Omri to reign over Israel, twelve years: . . . "
(I Kings 16:23).

Most people say, "Omri? I don't even remember ever hearing of him. When I read through the Bible, I just kind of skimmed through that part in a hurry." But Omri got the throne as the sixth king of the northern kingdom:

"But Omri wrought evil in the eyes of the LORD, and did worse than all that were before him"
(I Kings 16:25).

What Omri did was to move the capital of the northern kingdom from Tirzah—where Jeroboam I had established it—to Samaria. Omri bought a field from a man named Shemer, and built a city there called Samaria.

So Samaria became the capital of the northern kingdom—Israel—and remained so for a thousand years. Of course, the capital of the southern kingdom—Judah—was Jerusalem.

Then Omri went a little further. He said, "We need to have an alliance with the nations around us so that we won't have war. The best way to do that is to marry my children to the children of the leaders of those nations." Omri had a son named Ahab, and he married Ahab to a Zidonian woman named Jezebel.

"Jezebel and Ahab? Oh yes, I've heard of them!" Sure you have, but did you know where their curse got started? You've got to back it up a couple of generations or so to see that their wickedness was an inherited curse.

Jezebel was an awful woman. She was the daughter of Ethbaal, and she became a priestess to Baal. Now as the queen, she carried the whole nation of Israel into the worship of Baal. When she did that, God did all kinds of things to get to Ahab, but Ahab was a very, very weak man. He would lean toward God, and then he'd get back involved with his wife's idolatry again.

With each generation God never leaves them without a witness. He always gives them a chance to break the generation curse. God always wants to reverse the curse for them. So God begins to deal with Ahab, and He sends marvelous prophets to him.

Ahab and Elijah

God sent Elijah to Ahab over and over again, challenging him to repent of wickedness. God just keeps on dealing with people, and their own hardheartedness or their own weakness is usually what gets in the way. Ahab saw many miracles. He saw Elijah pray, and the heavens closed. He saw Elijah pray and, after three-and-a-half years of drought, he saw the heavens open again:

> *"And Ahab the son of Omri did evil in the sight of the LORD above all that were before him"* (I Kings 16:30).

Ahab saw many marvelous miracles, but he never really committed his life to God. He was worse than his father. You'll remember that "seven evil spirits" will come back with the next generation. It may have started out with only one evil spirit that plagued the father, but in the next generation he brought seven more—"... *more wicked than himself; ...*" (Luke 11:26).

Ahab and Micaiah

God sent Elijah—then He sent Micaiah (I Kings 22). Ahab was going out to battle, and he said, "I need a message from the Lord to be sure I'm really going to win." Ahab had persuaded Jehoshaphat, the king of the southern kingdom, to come up and be his ally. So Ahab said, "I'm going to call out my prophets."

Jehoshaphat agreed, "Yes, we need to have a confirmation from the Lord, so call up the prophets." Of course, all the prophets that Ahab had were prophets of Baal, and who knows what all they were involved in! They came up and prophesied, saying, "You'll win, you'll win!"

But Jehoshaphat—who was a godly man and who had no business being up there anyway—asked, "You know, I don't feel really good about this. Do you have any other prophets?"

Ahab answered, "Yes, I've got one in prison. I don't like the way he prophesies, so I just keep him in prison. He never says anything good about me."

Jehoshaphat insisted, "Go get him out of prison." So they dragged Micaiah up before the kings:

> *"And the king said unto him, How many times shall I adjure thee that thou tell me nothing but that which is true in the name of the LORD?"* (I Kings 22:16).

Ahab said, "I want you to prophesy." At first, Micaiah started to prophesy something kind, and Ahab interrupted him, "Now

Micaiah, I can tell you're just pretending. Come on, prophesy, really prophesy!"

Then Micaiah answered, "Well, you're going to be killed today."

Ahab got disgusted and said, "See, I told you that every time he prophesies he tells me something bad. I can't stand him, so throw him in jail again." So they threw Micaiah back in jail, but Ahab did get killed that day. Micaiah was a true prophet.

Ahaziah, the Careless King

So there was Omri, who did evil in the sight of God. Then there came Ahab, who was seven times more wicked than his father. But if you think Ahab and Jezebel were bad, they had a son named Ahaziah:

Ahaziah the son of Ahab began to reign over Israel in Samaria the seventeenth year of Jehoshaphat king of Judah, . . . And he did evil in the sight of the LORD, and walked in the way of his father, and in the way of his mother, and in the way of Jeroboam the son of Nebat, who made Israel to sin: For he served Baal, and worshipped him, and provoked to anger the LORD God of Israel, according to all that his father had done (I Kings 22:51-53).

Ahaziah came along, and he had a godly name, which meant "Jehovah sustains." But he was involved in idolatry just like his father and mother, and just like his grandfather. Here we have a generation curse. Idolatry is a generation curse . . . cruelty and violence are generation curses . . . sexual sin is a generation curse. Ahaziah was involved in each of these generation curses.

One day Ahaziah was walking in his big palace in Samaria. He was walking around, very pleased with himself: "I'm the great king. I'm everything." Of course, he thought nothing could touch him. Now in his palace there was a hallway with a beautiful lattice over a winding stairway. He looked through the lattice and leaned over to see if somebody was coming into the court.

He leaned too far, and he fell through the lattice. He fell down to the first floor, and he became very, very sick. He was so badly hurt that he said, "I'm concerned that I'm going to die." Then Ahaziah sent messengers out to his favorite idol, *Baal-zebub*—which means "god of the flies." Most of us are trying to get rid of flies, but back then they worshiped those stupid things:

> *But the angle of the LORD said to Elijah the Tishbite, Arise, go up to meet the messengers of the king of Samaria, and say unto them, Is it not because there is not a God in Israel, that ye go to enquire of Baal-zebub the god of Ekron?* (II Kings 1:3).

So Ahaziah sent messengers to Baal-zebub, but a prophet named Elijah stopped him. Elijah said, "Isn't there a God in Israel, that the king has to send to the god of the flies? There is a living God, and I'll give Ahaziah a message—go back and tell him he's going to die."

So the messengers went back to the king and said, "You are going to die." And Ahaziah died.

Joram and Elisha

After Ahaziah died, his brother Joram (also known as Jehoram) took the throne. We like to think, "Well, maybe this one will change, because this is still the third generation." But it doesn't change:

> *Now Jehoram the son of Ahab began to reign over Israel in Samaria the eighteenth year of Jehoshaphat king of Judah, and reigned twelve years. And he*

> *wrought evil in the sight of the LORD; but not like*
> *his father, and like his mother: for he put away the*
> *image of Baal that his father had made. Nevertheless*
> *he cleaved unto the sins of Jeroboam the son of*
> *Nebat, which made Israel to sin; he departed not*
> *therefrom* (II Kings 3:1-3).

Joram walked in idolatry and wickedness. He was worse than Omri, worse than Ahab, worse than Jezebel, worse than Ahaziah. He was involved in all kinds of sin. He decided to try and get Jehoshaphat, the king of the southern kingdom, to go in with him on some business venture. Therefore God sent another prophet.

With each generation, God sent a specific prophet to deal with the king, to get him to turn around and repent. If you look back on your life, you'll see many, many times when God tried to keep you out of sin. Maybe you stopped right at that point, or maybe someone came and dealt with you. God is so merciful; He constantly wants to break that thing. Remember: with each generation it is going to get worse and worse.

So Elisha came along just as Joram and Jehoshaphat were going to fight with the king of Moab. While they were on their way to the battlefield, they ran out of water. The cattle, the horses, and the men got hungry and thirsty, and it looked like they were going to perish before they ever fought the battle. Joram said, "Oh, God has brought us out here to kill us."

But Jehoshaphat said, "Wait a minute, isn't there a prophet around? Can't we do something?" At least Jehoshaphat knew to call on God for help.

The Israelites answered, "Yes, there is a man back there named Elisha who is a prophet."

"Well, send him up here!"

But Joram protested, "I don't like him too well. My brother fell through a lattice, and Elijah told him he would die, and he died. Elisha is just like Elijah":

> *"And Jehoshaphat said, The word of the LORD is with him. . . . "* (II Kings 3:12).

Jehoshaphat said, "Well, bring him up here anyway. I like him, and we need God's help."

So they brought Elisha up, and he had a message for the crowd. In His great mercy, God was dealing with Joram, trying to break the generation curse.

The prophet said, "Bring me a minstrel." When the minstrel began to play, Elisha got into the Spirit, and the Lord began to speak through him about the drought problem:

> *And he said, Thus saith the LORD, Make this valley full of ditches. For thus saith the LORD, Ye shall not see wind, neither shall ye see rain; yet that valley shall be filled with water, that ye may drink, both ye, and your cattle, and your beasts. And this is but a light thing in the sight of the LORD: he will deliver the Moabites also into your hand. And it came to pass in the morning, when the meat offering was offered, that, behold, there came water by the way of Edom, and the country was filled with water* (II Kings 3:16-18,20).

Elisha commanded, "Dig ditches because you're going to get a miracle." They dug the ditches, and they got the most unusual miracle: those little ditches were filled in the morning with water. The Bible said, "At the time of the morning sacrifice they filled up with water." So the people were able to drink.

But when the king of Moab came over the hill to fight, the sun shown on those little patches of water, and it looked like blood. It was like an optical illusion.

When the king of Moab looked at the blood, he said, "Oh, they've gotten into a fight and killed each other." He thought the battle was over before it had been fought! So the Moabites came running down the hill, ready to pick up the loot . . . and found the Israelites ready for battle. The Israelites had just refreshed themselves with the miracle water God had provided, and they were ready to fight! So they just wiped out the Moabites.

When Joram saw this tremendous miracle, you'd think that would stop him in his tracks and cause him to repent and return to the true and living God. But no, he just got more involved with idolatry. Finally, Joram was killed by Jehu.

Athaliah—Mixing Bad With Good

Joram had a sister, Athaliah, who was the daughter of Jezebel and Ahab. Athaliah was very evil. She was married to a man named Jehoram (also known as Joram) who was the king of the southern kingdom.

Now you say, "Oh no, that's the house of David. Those are the good kings!" This Jehoram was the son of Jehoshaphat, and Jehoshaphat was a good king. So Jehoram of the good lineage married Athaliah of the bad lineage, and the Word says:

"Can two walk together, except they be agreed?" (Amos 3:3).

Don't marry an unbeliever! You don't need their generation curses in your family; you've got enough curses in your own family to bind! Don't be stupid and run out and marry somebody who's not really committed to Jesus Christ. You may be bringing something into your home that's seven times worse than anything you could ever dream:

*. . . Jehoram the son of Jehoshaphat king of Judah
began to reign. Thirty and two years old was he
when he began to reign; and he reigned eight years
in Jerusalem. And he walked in the way of the kings
of Israel, as did the house of Ahab: for the daughter
of Ahab was his wife: and he did evil in the sight
of the LORD* (II Kings 8:16-18).

So Jehoram was married to Athaliah for eight years, and they
had several children. But then Jehoram was killed in a battle,
and their son, Ahaziah—yes, another Ahaziah—became the
king. This is now the fifth generation: Omri, Ahab, Ahaziah
(the one who fell through the lattice and died), and his brother
Joram, who are of the same lineage, then Athaliah (who married
a different Jehoram) and her son Ahaziah.

Now this Ahaziah had two things in him: he had a godly
heritage from Jehoshaphat, his paternal grandfather; but he
also had an ungodly heritage from Jezebel, his maternal grandmother, and Athaliah, his mother. He had a warring nature:

*"Train up a child in the way he should go: and when
he is old, he will not depart from it"* (Proverbs 22:6).

Mothers! You hold the key to your children's choices. Fathers
certainly set a godly example, but children invariably follow the
way their mothers lead. You must be a strong woman of prayer.
You must be daily in the Word, seeking wisdom and guidance
in influencing your children's lives. You will direct them when
they come to their crossroad:

*Behold, I set before you this day a blessing and a
curse; A blessing, if ye obey the commandments of the
LORD your God, which I command you this day: And
a curse, if ye will not obey the commandments of
the LORD your God, but turn aside out of the way
which I command you this day, to go after other gods,*

which ye have not known (Deuteronomy 11:26-28).

So Ahaziah took the throne, and he was very cruel:

> . . . *Ahaziah the son of Jehoram king of Judah begin to reign. . . . And his mother's name was Athaliah, . . . And he walked in the way of the house of Ahab, and did evil in the sight of the LORD, . . .* (II Kings 8:25-27).

Ahaziah was eventually killed in a battle, leaving children who were heirs to the throne. However, Athaliah wanted the throne. She was so evil that she killed her own grandchildren. Athaliah actually killed all her grandchildren with the exception of Joash.

Can you imagine that? If you are a grandparent, you know that your grandchildren are the delight of your life. You love your grandchildren! But this family was under a generation curse, and it was getting seven times worse with each generation. And I believe that murdering your grandchildren is certainly seven times worse:

> *And when Athaliah the mother of Ahaziah saw that her son was dead, she arose and destroyed all the seed royal. . . . And Athaliah did reign over the land* (II Kings 11:1,3).

So Athaliah murdered her grandchildren and put herself on the throne. She was the only woman who ever ruled on the throne of David, and she ruled for six years.

Joash, the Good King

Now if she had succeeded in murdering all of her grandchildren, the house of David would have ended. But God had promised David that his house would never end, and there would always be someone on his throne . . . and that Jesus would come through the house of David.

If Athaliah had murdered all of her grandchildren, that would mean there would not be a Messiah coming through the house of David. That would stop God's seed, and the devil knows these things. So he thought, "If I get these generations doing worse and worse things"—of course, God was dealing with each generation as it came along—"I can stop the Messiah of God to the earth!"

> *But Jehosheba . . . took Joash the son of Ahaziah, and stole him from among the king's sons which were slain; and they hid him, even him and his nurse, in the bedchamber from Athaliah, so that he was not slain. And he was with her hid in the house of the LORD six years. . . . (II Kings 11:2,3).*

Athaliah also had a daughter, named Jehosheba, who married a priest of the living God, named Jehoiada. The princess Jehosheba and the priest Jehoiada slipped in and sneaked out a baby named Joash (also known as Jehoash), one of Athaliah's grandchildren.

Athaliah had ordered them all to be murdered, but Joash didn't get killed. Her own daughter hid the boy! Any time you get somebody who turns to God, what happens? You reverse the curse!

Athaliah thought she had murdered them all. Do you see how close that thing came between the devil and God's seed? So Athaliah's daughter and son-in-law hid her grandson for six years:

> *And he brought forth the king's son, and put the crown upon him, and gave him the testimony; and they made him king, and anointed him; and they clapped their hands, and said, God save the king. And when Athaliah heard the noise of the guard and of the people, she came to the people into the temple*

> *of the LORD. And when she looked, behold, the king*
> *stood by a pillar, as the manner was, and the princes*
> *and the trumpeters by the king, and all the people*
> *of the land rejoiced, and blew with trumpets: and*
> *Athaliah rent her clothes, and cried, Treason, Treason.*
> *And they laid hands on her; and she went by the*
> *way by the which the horses came into the king's*
> *house: and there was she slain* (II Kings 11:12-14,16).

When Joash was seven years old—at the end of the sixth year of Athaliah's reign—Jehosheba and Jehoiada brought out this little boy, and they put him on the throne, saying, "God save the king!"

Then Athaliah comes running in—and I think of her with long, greasy, gray hair flying in the breeze—and she said, "Treason! Treason!" But they killed her. And that was the end of Omri's evil generation seed.

Joash was a good king. Why?

> *"And Jehoash did that which was right in the sight*
> *of the LORD all his days wherein Jehoiada the priest*
> *instructed him"* (II Kings 12:2).

Joash turned his life over to God. The generation curse was broken. Any time you come to the Lord, He takes the curse for you and actually reverses it. And the next king was good, too, and the throne of David was not ended because Jesus sits on the throne today!

Now there's one more family for us to look at.

Chapter Twelve
THE HERITAGE OF THE RECHABITES

And when he was departed thence, he lighted on Jehonadab the son of Rechab coming to meet him: and he saluted him, and said to him, Is thine heart right, as my heart is with thy heart? And Jehonadab answered, It is. . . . And Jehu went, and Jehonadab the son of Rechab, into the house of Baal, and said unto the worshippers of Baal, Search, and look that there be here with you none of the servants of the LORD, but the worshippers of Baal only (II Kings 10:15,23).

Jehonadab, the son of Rechab, lived in Israel in the day of Ahab and Jezebel. In spite of all the idolatry going on around him, Jehonadab loved God very much, and he hated what was going on. So he rebelled against Ahab and Jezebel.

As Ahab and Jezebel reigned over the northern kingdom, continuing to lead the people in idolatry, Jehonadab said, "I'm not going to have my children under the influence of idolatry and Baal worship," so he left the city of Samaria.

Jehonadab—The Man Who Responded to God

Then God spoke to him, "If you will be true to Me, there are three things I'm going to require of you: that you not drink anything of the vine; that you not buy any land; and that you

111

will be a nomad and make your living from goats and sheep. Teach your children this way, and I will protect your household, and they will never be involved in idolatry."

About this time there was civil war in Israel. Ahaziah became the king; but he had to fight to keep his throne. Then a man named Jehu came upon the scene. He had been anointed by Elisha to go into Israel and cut off the house of Ahab and take the northern kingdom's throne.

Jehu was the son of Jehoshaphat, the son of Nimshi; and one from the prophets' school anointed him king. So Jehu was anointed by God's prophet, and he had all the right people on his side.

Then Jehu came to Jehonadab and said, "Would you go with me and help me kill the priests of Baal and Jezebel?" And Jehonadab agreed:

> *And when Jehu was come to Jezreel, Jezebel heard of it; and she painted her face, and tired her head, and looked out at a window. And as Jehu entered in at the gate, she said, Had Zimri peace, who slew his master? And he lifted up his face to the window, and said, Who is on my side? who? And there looked out to him two or three eunuchs. Ad he said, Throw her down. So they threw her down: and some of her blood was sprinkled on the wall, and on the horses: and he trode her under foot* (II Kings 9:30-33).

As old as she was then, Jezebel still painted her eyes and arranged her hair, then she went to look out the palace window. She looked down at Jehu and asked, "What do you want?"

Jehu answered, "I want you to die."

Jezebel laughed, "Oh, you know what happened to the last

man who rebelled against the king."

But there were some eunuchs standing up there with her, and Jehu commanded, "Push her over." And they did. She fell, and the dogs of the city ate her body, except for the palms of her hands, just as had been prophesied.

Then Jehu went in and had dinner—can you imagine eating after that spectacle! Then they decided to bury what was left of Jezebel, giving her honors because she was a king's daughter. However, there was nothing to bury.

So here is Jehonadab, who had proven that he was true to God. God said to him, "If you will keep your generations correct—if you will teach each generation and the next generation and the next generation—then I will protect them from these curses. They shall not get into idolatry."

The way we live is serious. What we do affects our children and our grandchildren. Once the curses are broken, we must continue in God in order to keep the curses broken. When we walk in righteousness, the next generation and the next generation are going to be blessed because of us. The earth will be blessed because we're here now because *"Righteousness exalteth a nation: . . . "* (Proverbs 14:34).

The People Who Remained Faithful to God

Go unto the house of the Rechabites, and speak unto them, and bring them into the house of the LORD, into one of the chambers, . . . And Jeremiah said unto the house of the Rechabites, Thus saith the LORD of hosts, the God of Israel; Because ye have obeyed the commandment of Jonadab [Jehonadab] *your father, and kept all his precepts, and done according unto all that he hath commanded you: Therefore thus saith the LORD of hosts, the God of Israel; Jonadab the son of Rechab shall*

113

not want a man to stand before me for ever (Jeremiah 35:2,18,19).

Years later Jeremiah (called the "weeping prophet") was down in the southern kingdom, crying and weeping over Judah because they'd gone astray.

One day God told Jeremiah, "Call in the princes of Judah, and call in the Rechabites." That's Jehonadab's people because he was the son of Rechab. The Rechabites were Jehonadab's children and grandchildren, several generations later. God told Jeremiah, "Call in the Rechabites and pour wine for all of them. Have the princes of Judah come in and watch"(Jeremiah 35).

So Jeremiah called in all the Rechabites and seated them at a table of honor. He poured wine for each of them.

"Now wait a minute, Marilyn! Didn't God tell Jehonadab that his seed were not to drink wine?" That's right. There were three things God commanded Jehonadab and his seed: they were not to drink wine; they were not to buy land; and they were to be nomads.

"So what was Jeremiah doing when he poured wine for them? These were godly people, and he was a prophet! Why was he tempting them?"

God was teaching a lesson to two groups of people that day: to the Rechabites and to the princes of Judah who had gone astray. Jeremiah poured the wine for the Rechabites right in front of the Judaean princes and said, "Go ahead, you sons of Jehonadab, have a drink."

But they answered, "No, we can't drink. We have a vow to God. We're going to serve God from generation to generation. We're not going to drink wine, not even a little friendly glass on special occasions. And we're not going to own land, and we're going to continue to be a nomadic people."

Jeremiah smiled one of his rare smiles and said, "But go ahead, have a drink! I've poured it for you already."

The Rechabites answered, "No, we can't."

Then Jeremiah turned to the princes of Judah and said, "Do you see these people? They made a family promise to serve God. They're going to serve Him no matter what happens. They are just the seed of Jehonadab, but they're remaining faithful to God.

"However, you are the seed of David, and you're breaking all of the laws that God has given, the laws that are to be a blessing to your generations! You're turning your blessings into curses!"

Jeremiah said, "How could you turn your blessings into curses? These people have been true to God in their simple way. Why can't you be true to the way of God Himself, so that the Messiah can come through your seed?"

Jeremiah showed the Rechabites as an example to the princes of Judah, but they still did not yield.

The Rechabites really had the right idea. They refused to yield to pressure, even when it seemed to be coming from a righteous source (yes, they were tested). They refused to submit to alcohol. They wouldn't even be "social drinkers."

Do you know that alcohol destroys your brain cells? You need all of your brain cells! No one is so smart that he can stand to lose a few. Wally and I have seen people who once were brilliant become mental vegetables because they became alcoholics.

Parents who are social drinkers set a double standard for their children. They say to their children, "Now don't drink." But then the children see their folks laughing it up with a glass of wine or a can of beer in their hands. Parents: don't teach your children not to drink when you do it. You don't want your child to be an alcoholic, so throw those wine bottles out!

The Promises of God Are Everlasting

Now back to the Rechabites. After Jeremiah admonished the princes of Judah, he turned and prophesied to the children of Jehonadab. He said, "Because you have been true to God, when Nebuchadnezzar comes in here and destroys Judah, he will not take you captive. Your children will be free, and your grandchildren will be free. They will never go into captivity."

Then he prophesied to the princes of Judah, "But you princes of Judah! Your children will be eunuchs. They will be taken into captivity and murdered. They will be killed, and you will have no generation because you would not judge yourselves and judge your sin."

God's final word to the sons of Jehonadab: "You shall never lack a descendant to stand before Me!" Isn't that a beautiful promise?

Now let me tell you what happened to the Rechabites. While they lived in the northern kingdom, Assyria came down and attacked Israel. The Assyrians took all the people captive except the Rechabites because they weren't there! They were nomads, and they had gone down to Judah at that time because of a famine. They were safe with all their sheep, and their lambs, and their oxen. They missed the Assyrian captivity! Now that's divine protection.

Then years later, Nebuchadnezzar attacked Judah. "Oh well, there go the Rechabites." No, that's not what happened.

When Nebuchadnezzar conquered Judah, he told his soldiers, "Leave the nomads alone." So the Rechabites were never taken into captivity by the Assyrians or by the Babylonians.

The seed of Jehonadab didn't fall apart because they were true to God. "You can't curse what God has blessed!" If you are walking in the Word of God, then you are walking in the blessings of God, and there can't be a curse come upon you or your generations. You're not here to be cursed because you are here to reverse the curse!

The Promise Still Works Today

Now I've saved the best part for last. Do you know that there are Rechabites living in Jericho today? The Rechabites have not ended, and they are still serving the God of their fathers. That's generation after generation after generation after generation of blessed people! God said, "Those that love Me, I will bless them to the thousandth generation!" The Rechabites are living proof that serving God and walking in His Word brings a blessing into your life and continues that blessing on down through your generations, breaking the curse of the past!

Chapter Thirteen
THE HOUSE OF RIGHTEOUSNESS

So you want to be free from generation curses, and you want to clean up your act right now. You're willing to forgive those who have gone before you and passed down their curses to you. You're willing to forgive those people who have hurt you today, and you're going to pray for them rather than be bitter against them. You want your children and your children's children to inherit only blessings from you.

Watch Out for These!

"He that troubleth his own house shall inherit the wind: . . . " (Proverbs 11:29).

I used to think, " 'Inheriting the wind' means that you get an empty handful of nothing. You cannot hold onto wind." But I've since learned that if you are violent to your wife or cruel to your children or hateful with your mouth, if you are ugly and gripe about the things of God, then you are going to inherit the wind . . . but it will be a hurricane:

Therefore whosoever heareth these sayings of mine, and doeth them, I will liken him unto a wise man, which built his house upon a rock: And the rain descended, and the floods came, and the winds blew, and beat upon that house; and it fell not: for it was founded upon a rock.

119

> *And every one that heareth these sayings of mine,*
> *and doeth them not, shall be likened unto a foolish*
> *man, which built his house upon the sand: And the*
> *rain descended, and the floods came, and the winds*
> *blew, and beat upon that house; and it fell: and great*
> *was the fall of it* (Matthew 7:24-27).

If your house is built on sand and not on the Word, then it's going to blow down. Don't gripe at God. Don't gripe at the church. Don't gripe at other Christians because in so doing you are troubling your own house:

> *"He that is greedy of gain troubleth his own*
> *house; . . . "* (Proverbs 15:27).

What does that mean? "Greedy of gain" is idolatry. It's saying, "I'd rather make money than go to church . . . I'd rather make money than go to early morning prayer." This refers to what your true priorities are:

> *"But seek ye first the kingdom of God, and his*
> *righteousness; and all these things shall be added*
> *unto you"* (Matthew 6:33).

If the pursuit of riches and wealth is more important to you than seeking first the kingdom of God, then you are into idolatry . . . and idolatry is a terrible sin.

Do you remember what God said would happen to idolaters?

> *Thou shalt have none other gods before me. Thou*
> *shalt not bow down thyself unto them, nor serve*
> *them: for I the LORD thy God am a jealous God,*
> *visiting the iniquity of the fathers upon the children*
> *unto the third and fourth generation of them that*
> *hate me* (Deuteronomy 5:7,9).

What kind of curse does idolatry bring?

> *But it shall come to pass, if thou wilt not hearken unto the voice of the LORD thy God, . . . The LORD shall send upon thee cursing, vexation, and rebuke, in all that thou settest thine hand unto for to do, until thou be destroyed, and until thou perish quickly; because of the wickedness of thy doings, whereby thou hast forsaken me* (Deuteronomy 28:15,20).

Is that scary enough? No? Then try this:

> *The LORD shall make the pestilence cleave unto thee, until he have consumed thee from off the land, . . . The LORD shall smite thee with a consumption, and with a fever, and with an inflammation, and with an extreme burning, and with the sword, and with blasting, and with mildew; and they shall pursue thee until thou perish* (Deuteronomy 28:21,22).

These are the sort of curses that come upon you if you turn to idolatry . . . and they will come upon your children and upon your children's children too! Now that's scary!

Another form of idolatry is the pursuit of fame and power. "I want an important position." The lust for power is idolatry. Don't you know that true recognition comes from the Lord:

> *"But God is the judge: he putteth down one, and setteth up another"* (Psalms 75:7).

> *"So then it is not of him that willeth, nor of him that runneth, but of God that sheweth mercy"* (Romans 9:16).

If you spend your time trying to gain public acceptance and popularity, then you're going to see a backlash in your own family. Chasing fame is idolatry, and the curse of that sin is going to overtake you.

It's going to overtake your children and your generations

because they will inherit your weakness. They will be prey to the familiar spirits that are just watching and waiting for their turn to strike at the next generation. And most likely your children will be seven times worse than you are:

> *"Whoso rewardeth evil for good, evil shall not depart from his house"* (Proverbs 17:13).

That means that if you work for a good employer, but you sow evil back, watch out! Remember what Paul wrote about that:

> *"And whatsoever ye do, do it heartily, as to the Lord, and not unto men"* (Colossians 3:23).

"Well, I just don't like that person." It doesn't matter if you like that person or not—if you reward evil for good, then you're bringing a curse in. If those people have been good to you, and have not talked against you, but then you turn around and talk against them—watch out!

When Wally and I were assistant pastors of a church in Amarillo, Texas, we got into a situation with the church secretary. She blabbed too much, and she was bitter about some things.

Wally and I were young, and this was our first time in the ministry. This woman began telling us things, and we started sucking all that stuff into our spirits, into our minds, and into our emotions. Then we started talking.

When God called us out to have a church, pretty soon I noticed some people were doing to us what we had done to the other pastor. Do you know what I did? I repented! I said, "I will never disrespect the hand that feeds me. I will never do that again!"

That pastor hadn't hurt us any; he was good to us. But I learned never to reward evil for good by picking up somebody else's offenses. That's a sin, and it brings a curse on me and on my household. You know that I repented! When I saw that man later, I could look him full in his face and think, "I'm clean! Glory to God, I'm clean!"

Strive For These!

" . . . *the house of the righteous shall stand"* (Proverbs 12:7).

That's what we're trying to achieve! We are *"the righteousness of God in him* [Christ]" (II Corinthians 5:21). We are freed from the generation curses, and we shall stand:

"Through wisdom is an house builded; . . . " (Proverbs 24:3).

What you are gaining through this teaching can build your house. You won't be building your house on sand, but on the Rock of the Word of God. You will be doing what God called you to do.

A Word to Women . . .

"Every wise woman buildeth her house: but the foolish plucketh it down with her hands" (Proverbs 14:1).

Ladies: what do you say to your children about their father? Do you say, "I wish he made more money . . . I wish he weren't so fat . . . I wish he'd fix all these things that are broken around here . . . I wish he'd do something about his car—I'm tired of this old wreck . . . I wish he'd go to church, that big thug!"

If that's the way you talk about your husband to your children, then you're not a wise woman. You've got bitterness in your heart, and you're pouring it onto your children.

Maybe you've been divorced, and you're deeply wounded by your former spouse. Do you want to pour that bitterness out onto your children? Do you know what will happen? Your little girl is going to pour out the same bitterness on her husband and have a divorce just like you had.

This is a real battle! We're dealing with serious things. This isn't a cupcake factory or an old people's home or a country club . . . this is spiritual warfare! If we fight the battle God's way, then there will be some wonderful victories:

> *"Let all bitterness, and wrath, and anger, . . . be put away from you, . . . "* (Ephesians 4:31).

Why? Because when you eat it, it's sour grapes—you'll set your children's teeth on edge, and you'll start a generation curse. Repent of it! Get free from it!

Don't pour your hurts and wounds out on your children—pour them out on Jesus, and let Him heal you. Then pour out love and wisdom on your kids. By wisdom the house is built.

. . . and a Word to Men

> *"Husbands, love your wives, and be not bitter against them"* (Colossians 3:19).

Why is it so bad to be bitter against your wife? What do you think about your wife? "That fat slob . . . I wish she could make a decent gravy, like my mother . . . I wish she were a better Christian . . . I wish she'd get to be more of a fanatic about the way she keeps the house like she is a fanatic about church . . . I wish she were a better lover."

Well, maybe you need to be a better lover! Do you ever tell her that you love her and that she looks good?

Husband, don't be bitter against your wife, because you defile yourself. You defile your home, and you'll defile your son for his marriage if that's the way you talk. You'll start a generation curse because you've eaten sour grapes, and you'll set your children and your grandchildren's teeth on edge.

Bitterness is a luxury, and you can't afford it. It costs too much. It costs your children, and it costs your grandchildren. Whoever you are bitter against, you'd better forgive them and get rid of it!

The Right Way

Now let me tell you something not to do: don't run up to somebody at church and say, "I've been bitter against you for months; please forgive me," and they didn't even know it!

Then they think, "My, my! What did I do?" You walk away all forgiven, and they become heartsick. If someone doesn't know he's offended you, then shut up and go to God. Don't make another problem.

But if the person does know about it, and you've been ugly with him, then it doesn't matter what he's done—you get free before God, and you get free before him! Job got free with both God and man, and then his captivity was turned.

The Best Attitude

" . . . to the hungry soul every bitter thing is sweet" (Proverbs 27:7).

If you are hungry for God, then you will not get bitter. You will make the bitter sweet. If you're hungry for God, and somebody is mean to you, you'll say, "Well God, here's Your opportunity to make my *friend* at peace with me, because *"When a man's ways please the LORD, he maketh even his enemies to be at peace with him"* (Proverbs 16:7).

"You're calling him a *friend?*"

Yes, that "enemy" is a friend "to the hungry soul," to the man or woman who is hungry after God. Do you know what happens to the "hungry soul" when a trial comes? He thinks that God is getting ready to give him a bigger miracle!

Are you in a financial trial? Then praise God—and don't get bitter—because you're about to get a miracle! You make the choice. You decide what is going to happen to you, whether you're going to continue with this attack on your finances— maybe it's a generation curse trying to latch onto you—or if you're going to stop the devil in his tracks.

Curses Into Blessings

The biggest miracles in my life didn't come out of everything just going smoothly. People weren't saying, "That Marilyn Hickey, isn't she just great!" No, they were saying, "What is she doing? She must be crazy!" Why? Because during the time of what has probably been the greatest financial trial our ministry has ever faced, it was then that God opened the door for us to go on daily television.

When the financial pressure was on, the devil was hitting us with strife and everything under the sun, and I thought, "God, where is the nearest bridge? I'll shoot myself and just fall over backwards so I can't miss."

But God kept telling me, "Hang in with Me. Stay in the Spirit, and you will get a miracle!"

It was during that time that God gave us the biggest miracle we've ever had in our ministry. Why? Because " . . . *to the hungry soul every bitter thing is sweet,*" and God knows how to reverse the curse!

The answer wasn't for me to quit. The answer was for me to say, "God, I'm so hungry for You. What miracle do YOU have?" So I watched Him come on the scene and do something just out of this world!

Freedom From Cancer

There are all sorts of generation curses we haven't dealt with yet. One of the biggies is cancer.

If you have a family history of cancer, then join me out loud right now in prayer as we break that curse of cancer:

Dear heavenly Father, I come to You in the name of Jesus. I thank You that Jesus paid that price, that Jesus took the cancer, and I don't have to have it. I reverse the curse in Jesus' name. My children will never have cancer, and their children will never have cancer, and their grandchildren will never have cancer. The curse is broken! In Jesus' name, Amen.

Now thank Him every day of your life that He already paid the price, He already shed His blood, and you won't ever be subject to cancer. The more often you speak that word of positive confession, the more often the devil will also hear you saying it to the Father . . . and he'll not be able to get an inroad into your life or in your children's lives.

Oh, yes, the devil can hear you standing on God's Word! He can hear you praising Jesus every day for breaking the curse of cancer from your life. It makes him so mad because he was that "strong man" whose house was taken back from him, and he's looking for a place to reside. But he also hears you saying, "My children are not under that curse anymore either." And that probably makes him madder!

Staying Free

But don't put up with the devil's junk. If he comes with symptoms of something that you've broken, you need to go at him again! One mistake Christians make is thinking they only have one battle. That's a mistake. The devil will come at you with the same thing; you'll get free from the symptoms, and he'll come back again:

" *. . . greater is he that is in you, than he that is in the world*" (I John 4:4).

You've got to blast him with the Word and with your faith.

127

You may have to use it on your children. Say, "This is what the Word says . . . this is what the Word says!" You keep on fighting the enemy until you win. You don't give up—you stay with it.

You can be free from any curse that has invaded your life. You don't have to continue under the curse that your father or your grandfather or your great-grandfather sent down to your generation. Your children don't have to be under any of the curses either. You can break the generation curse today . . . right now . . . by the blood of Jesus Christ! You can reverse the curse, turning it into a blessing that will continue *"to the thousandth generation"*! Do it now!

Chapter Fourteen
ACTION: CURSES AND BLESSINGS

The Curse: General Ill Health

The Blessing:

"He sent his word, and healed them, and delivered them from their destructions" (Psalms 107:20).

"Surely he hath borne our griefs, and carried our sorrows: . . . But he was wounded for our transgressions, he was bruised for our iniquities: the chastisement of our peace was upon him; and with his stripes we are healed" (Isaiah 53:4,5).

" . . . let the weak say, I am strong" (Joel 3:10).

"Beloved, I wish above all things that thou mayest prosper and be in health, even as thy soul prospereth" (III John 2).

"Who his own self bare our sins in his own body on the tree, that we, being dead to sins, should live unto righteousness: by whose stripes ye were healed" (I Peter 2:24).

The Curse: Abdominal Pain

The Blessing:

"Be not wise in thine own eyes: fear the LORD, and depart from evil. It shall be health to thy navel, and marrow to thy bones" (Proverbs 3:7,8).

The Curse: Adultery

The Blessing:

"Marriage is honourable in all, and the bed undefiled: but whoremongers and adulterers God will judge" (Hebrews 13:4).

" . . . reproofs of instruction are the way of life: To keep thee from the evil woman, from the flattery of the tongue of a strange woman. Lust not after her beauty in thine heart; . . . " (Proverbs 6:23-25).

The Curse: Alcoholism

The Blessing:

"O taste and see that the LORD is good: blessed is the man that trusteth in him" (Psalms 34:8).

" . . . If any man thirst, let him come unto me, and drink" (John 7:37).

"Jesus answered and said unto her, Whosoever drinketh of this water shall thirst again: But whosoever drinketh of the water that I shall give him shall never thirst; but the water that I shall give him shall be in him a well of water springing up into everlasting life" (John 4:13,14).

"Then they cried unto the LORD in their trouble, and he delivered them out of their distresses" (Psalms 107:6).

"And it shall come to pass, that whosoever shall call on the name of the LORD shall be delivered: . . . " (Joel 2:32).

"If the Son therefore shall make you free, ye shall be free indeed" (John 8:36).

"For the law of the Spirit of life in Christ Jesus hath made me free from the law of sin and death" (Romans 8:2).

The Curse: Arthritis

The Blessing:

"Behold, thou hast instructed many, and thou hast strengthened the weak hands. Thy words have upholden him that was falling, and thou hast strengthened the feeble knees" (Job 4:3,4).

"Wherefore lift up the hands which hang down, and the feeble knees; And make straight paths for your feet, lest that which is lame be turned out of the way; but let it rather be healed" (Hebrews 12:12,13).

The Curse: Asthma and Colds

The Blessing:

"Why art thou cast down, O my soul? and why art thou disquieted within me? hope thou in God: for I shall yet praise him, who is the health of my countenance, and my God" (Psalms 42:11).

" . . . *seeing he giveth to all life, and breath, and all things*" (Acts 17:25).

The Curse: Argumentative Nature

The Blessing:

"*How forcible are right words! but what doth your arguing reprove?*" (Job 6:25).

The Curse: Back Pain

The Blessing:

"*The* LORD *upholdeth all that fall, and raiseth up all those that be bowed down*" (Psalms 145:14).

The Curse: Backsliding

The Blessing:

"*These things have I written unto you that believe on the name of the Son of God; that ye may know that ye have eternal life, . . .* " (I John 5:13).

" . . . *I know whom I have believed, and am persuaded that he is able to keep that which I have committed unto him against that day*" (II Timothy 1:12).

"*Hereby know we that we dwell in him, and he in us, because he hath given us of his Spirit*" (I John 4:13).

"*The Spirit itself beareth witness with our spirit, that we are the children of God*" (Romans 8:16).

The Curse: Blood Disease (Leukemia, Abnormal Blood Pressure, Diabetes)

The Blessing:

" . . . *I said unto thee when thou wast in thy blood, Live; yea, I said unto thee when thou wast in thy blood, Live"* (Ezekiel 16:6).

"Behold, I will bring it health and cure, and I will cure them, and will reveal unto them the abundance of peace and truth" (Jeremiah 33:6).

"Confess your faults one to another, and pray one for another, that ye may be healed. The effectual fervent prayer of a righteous man availeth much" (James 5:16).

"For I will cleanse their blood that I have not cleansed: . . . " (Joel 3:21).

The Curse: Bone Disease

The Blessing:

"Pleasant words are as an honeycomb, sweet to the soul, and health to the bones" (Proverbs 16:24).

"Have mercy upon me, O LORD; for I am weak: O LORD, heal me; for my bones are vexed" (Psalms 6:2).

The Curse: Broken Bones

The Blessing:

"He keepeth all his bones: not one of them is broken" (Psalms 34:20).

The Curse: Burns

The Blessing:

" . . . when thou walkest through the fire, thou shalt not be burned; neither shall the flame kindle upon thee" (Isaiah 43:2).

" . . . the LORD is thy shade upon thy right hand. The sun shall not smite thee by day, nor the moon by night" (Psalms 121:5,6).

The Curse: Cancer

The Blessing:

"For verily I say unto you, That whosoever shall say unto this mountain, Be thou removed, and be thou cast into the sea; and shall not doubt in his heart, but shall believe that those things which he saith shall come to pass; he shall have whatsoever he saith. Therefore I say unto you, What things soever ye desire, when ye pray, believe that ye receive them, and ye shall have them" (Mark 11:23,24).

" . . . Every plant, which my heavenly Father hath not planted, shall be rooted up" (Matthew 15:13).

The Curse: Condemnation

The Blessing:

"There is therefore now no condemnation to them which are in Christ Jesus, . . . " (Romans 8:1).

The Curse: Demonic Attack

The Blessing:

"Wherefore take unto you the whole armour of God, that ye may be able to withstand in the evil day, and having done all, to stand. Stand therefore, having your loins girt about with truth, and having on the breastplate of righteousness; And your feet shod with the preparation of the gospel of peace; Above all, taking the shield of faith, wherewith ye shall be able to quench all the fiery darts of the wicked. And take the helmet of salvation, and the sword of the Spirit, which is the word of God: Praying always with all prayer and supplication in the Spirit, . . . " (Ephesians 6:13-18).

The Curse: Dishonesty

The Blessing:

"Providing for honest things, not only in the sight of the Lord, but also in the sight of men" (II Corinthians 8:21).

"Neither give place to the devil" (Ephesians 4:27).

"Recompense to no man evil for evil. Provide things honest in the sight of all men" (Romans 12:17).

"Create in me a clean heart, O God; and renew a right spirit within me" (Psalms 51:10).

The Curse: Eye and Ear Problems

The Blessing:

"The LORD openeth the eyes of the blind: . . . " (Psalms 146:8).

"And the eyes of them that see shall not be dim, and the ears of them that hear shall hearken" (Isaiah 32:3).

"And in that day shall the deaf hear the words of the book, and the eyes of the blind shall see out of obscurity, and out of darkness" (Isaiah 29:18).

"Then the eyes of the blind shall be opened, and the ears of the deaf shall be unstopped" (Isaiah 35:5).

"The blind receive their sight, . . . and the deaf hear, . . . " (Matthew 11:5).

The Curse: Fatigue, Infirmity, Weakness

The Blessing:

"He giveth power to the faint; and to them that have no might he increaseth strength. But they that wait upon the LORD shall renew their strength; . . . " (Isaiah 40:29,31).

"Though I walk in the midst of trouble, thou wilt revive me: thou shalt stretch forth thine hand . . . and thy right hand shall save me" (Psalms 138:7).

" . . . but the spirit giveth life" (II Corinthians 3:6).

The Curse: Fearfulness, Shyness

The Blessing:

"I can do all things through Christ which strengtheneth me" (Philippians 4:13).

"... greater is he that is in you, than he that is in the world" (I John 4:4).

"But ye shall receive power, after that the Holy Ghost is come upon you: and ye shall be witnesses unto me ... " (Acts 1:8).

"The wicked flee when no man pursueth: but the righteous are bold as a lion" (Proverbs 28:1).

"... the people that do know their God shall be strong, and do exploits" (Daniel 11:32).

The Curse: Fear of Man

The Blessing:

"Nay, in all these things we are more than conquerors through him that loved us" (Romans 8:37).

"In God I will praise his word, in God I have put my trust; I will not fear what flesh can do unto me" (Psalms 56:4).

The Curse: Fear of Old Age

The Blessing:

"Bless the LORD, O my soul: and all that is within me, bless his holy name. Bless the LORD, O my soul, and forget not all his benefits: Who forgiveth all thine iniquities; who healeth

all thy diseases; Who redeemeth thy life from destruction; who crowneth thee with lovingkindness and tender mercies; Who satisfieth thy mouth with good things; so that thy youth is renewed like the eagle's" (Psalms 103:1-5).

"The righteous . . . shall still bring forth fruit in old age; they shall be fat and flourishing" (Psalms 92:12,14).

The Curse: Feet Trouble

The Blessing:

"For thou hast delivered my soul from death, mine eyes from tears, and my feet from falling. I will walk before the LORD in the land of the living" (Psalms 116:8,9).

"Then shalt thou walk in thy way safely, and thy foot shall not stumble" (Proverbs 3:23).

The Curse: Foolish Speech

The Blessing:

"Whoso keepeth his mouth and his tongue keepeth his soul from troubles" (Proverbs 21:23).

"For he that will love life, and see good days, let him refrain his tongue from evil, and his lips that they speak no guile" (I Peter 3:10).

"He that hath knowledge spareth his words: . . ." (Proverbs 17:27).

"In the multitude of words there wanteth not sin: but he that refraineth his lips is wise" (Proverbs 10:19).

"A man hath joy by the answer of his mouth: and a word spoken in due season, how good is it!" (Proverbs 15:23).

"Let no corrupt communication proceed out of your mouth, but that which is good to the use of edifying, that it may minister grace unto the hearers" (Ephesians 4:29).

"Let your speech be alway with grace, seasoned with salt, that ye may know how ye ought to answer every man" (Colossians 4:6).

"Set a watch, O LORD, before my mouth; keep the door of my lips" (Psalms 141:3).

The Curse: Foolishness

The Blessing:

"But of him are ye in Christ Jesus, who of God is made unto us wisdom, . . . " (I Corinthians 1:30).

The Curse: Hand Problems

The Blessing:

"Strengthen ye the weak hands, and confirm the feeble knees" (Isaiah 35:3).

The Curse: Hatefulness

The Blessing:

" . . . love one another; as I have loved you, that ye also love one another" (John 13:34).

"... the love of God is shed abroad in our hearts by the Holy Ghost ..." (Romans 5:5).

The Curse: Headaches and Migraines

The Blessing:

"But if the Spirit of him that raised up Jesus from the dead dwell in you, he that raised up Christ from the dead shall also quicken your mortal bodies by his Spirit that dwelleth in you" (Romans 8:11).

"This is my comfort in my affliction: for thy word hath quickened me" (Psalms 119:50).

The Curse: Heart Disease

The Blessing:

"Wait on the LORD: be of good courage, and he shall strengthen thine heart: wait, I say, on the LORD" (Psalms 27:14).

"The LORD is my strength and my shield; my heart trusted in him, and I am helped: therefore my heart greatly rejoiceth; and with my song will I praise him" (Psalms 28:7).

"Be of good courage, and he shall strengthen your heart, all ye that hope in the LORD" (Psalms 31:24).

"Keep thy heart with all diligence; for out of it are the issues of life" (Proverbs 4:23).

"A merry heart doeth good like a medicine: but a broken spirit drieth the bones" (Proverbs 17:22).

The Curse: Inferiority Complex

The Blessing:

"... *yet not I, but Christ liveth in me:* ... " (Galatians 2:20).

"... *I know whom I have believed, and am persuaded that he is able* ... " (II Timothy 1:12).

"... *If God be for us, who can be against us?"* (Romans 8:31).

"*So that we may boldly say, The Lord is my helper, and I will not fear what man shall do unto me"* (Hebrews 13:6).

"*Not that we are sufficient of ourselves to think any thing as of ourselves; but our sufficiency is of God"* (II Corinthians 3:5).

"*Whoso offereth praise glorifieth me:* ... " (Psalms 50:23).

"*This know also, that in the last days perilous times shall come. For men shall be lovers of their own selves, covetous, boasters, proud, blasphemers, disobedient to parents, unthankful, unholy"* (II Timothy 3:1,2).

"*Giving thanks always for all things unto God and the Father in the name of our Lord Jesus Christ"* (Ephesians 5:20).

"*By him therefore let us offer the sacrifice of praise to God continually,* ... " (Hebrews 13:15).

"*In every thing give thanks: for this is the will of God in Christ Jesus concerning you"* (I Thessalonians 5:18).

"*As ye have therefore received Christ Jesus the Lord, so walk ye in him: Rooted and built up in him, and stablished in the faith, as ye have been taught, abounding therein with thanksgiving"* (Colossians 2:6,7).

The Curse: Infertility

The Blessing:

" . . . there shall not be male or female barren among you, . . . " (Deuteronomy 7:14).

"He maketh the barren woman to keep house, and to be a joyful mother of children" (Psalms 113:9).

The Curse: Insomnia

The Blessing:

"I will both lay me down in peace, and sleep: for thou, LORD, only makest me dwell in safety" (Psalms 4:8).

"It is vain for you to rise up early, to sit up late, to eat the bread of sorrows: for so he giveth his beloved sleep" (Psalms 127:2).

"For the LORD hath poured out upon you the spirit of deep sleep, and hath closed your eyes: . . . " (Isaiah 29:10).

"When thou liest down, thou shalt not be afraid: yea, thou shalt lie down, and thy sleep shall be sweet" (Proverbs 3:24).

The Curse: Lack of Faith

The Blessing:

" . . . *God hath dealt to every man the measure of faith*" (Romans 12:3).

The Curse: Mental Disorder

The Blessing:

"*In the multitude of my thoughts within me thy comforts delight my soul*" (Psalms 94:19).

"*The LORD also will be a refuge for the oppressed, a refuge in times of trouble*" (Psalms 9:9).

"*Commit thy works unto the LORD, and thy thoughts shall be established*" (Proverbs 16:3).

" . . . *But we have the mind of Christ*" (I Corinthians 2:16).

"*Casting down imaginations, and every high thing that exalteth itself against the knowledge of God, and bringing into captivity every thought to the obedience of Christ*" (II Corinthians 10:5).

"*And the peace of God, which passeth all understanding, shall keep your hearts and minds through Christ Jesus*" (Philippians 4:7).

"*For God hath not given us the spirit of fear; but of power, and of love, and of a sound mind*" (II Timothy 1:7).

The Curse: Mouth, Lip, Tongue Problems

The Blessing:

"Whoso keepeth his mouth and his tongue keepeth his soul from troubles" (Proverbs 21:23).

"And straightway his ears were opened, and the string of his tongue was loosed, and he spake plain. And were beyond measure astonished, saying, He hath done all things well: he maketh both the deaf to hear, and the dumb to speak" (Mark 7:35,37).

"The mouth of a righteous man is a well of life: . . . " (Proverbs 10:11).

"He that keepeth his mouth keepeth his life: but he that openeth wide his lips shall have destruction" (Proverbs 13:3).

The Curse: Muscular Dystrophy and Multiple Sclerosis

The Blessing:

"There shall no evil befall thee, neither shall any plague come nigh thy dwelling. For he shall give his angels charge over thee, to keep thee in all thy ways. They shall bear thee up in their hands, lest thou dash thy foot against a stone" (Psalms 91:10-12).

The Curse: Negative Self-image

The Blessing:

"Do ye look on things after the outward appearance? If any man trust to himself that he is Christ's, let him of himself think

this again, that, as he is Christ's, even so are we Christ's"
(II Corinthians 10:7).

"Herein is our love made perfect, that we may have boldness
in the day of judgment: because as he is, so are we in this
world" (I John 4:17).

The Curse: Nervous Condition

The Blessing:

"God is our refuge and strength, a very present help in trouble"
(Psalms 46:1).

"Cast thy burden upon the LORD, and he shall sustain thee:
he shall never suffer the righteous to be moved" (Psalms 55:22).

" . . . where the Spirit of the Lord is, there is liberty"
(II Corinthians 3:17).

The Curse: Occult Practices

The Blessing:

"Wherefore God also hath highly exalted him, and given him
a name which is above every name: That at the name of Jesus
every knee should bow, of things in heaven, and things in earth,
and things under the earth: And that every tongue should
confess that Jesus Christ is Lord, to the glory of God the
Father" (Philippians 2:9-11).

"Submit yourselves therefore to God. Resist the devil, and he
will flee from you" (James 4:7).

"Lest Satan should get an advantage of us: for we are not ignorant of his devices" (II Corinthians 2:11).

"Behold, I give unto you power to tread on serpents and scorpions, and over all the power of the enemy: and nothing shall by any means hurt you" (Luke 10:19).

"... When the enemy shall come in like a flood, the Spirit of the LORD shall lift up a standard against him" (Isaiah 59:19).

"And ought not this woman, being a daughter of Abraham, whom Satan hath bound, lo, these eighteen years, be loosed from this bond on the sabbath day?" (Luke 13:16).

"Put on the whole armour of God, that ye may be able to stand against the wiles of the devil. For we wrestle not against flesh and blood, but against principalities, against powers, against the rulers of the darkness of this world, against spiritual wickedness in high places" (Ephesians 6:11,12).

The Curse: Oppression

The Blessing:

"Stand fast therefore in the liberty wherewith Christ hath made us free, and be not entangled again with the yoke of bondage" (Galatians 5:1).

"And it shall come to pass in that day, that his burden shall be taken away from off thy shoulder, and his yoke from off thy neck, and the yoke shall be destroyed because of the anointing" (Isaiah 10:27).

"The LORD is my light and my salvation; whom shall I fear?

the LORD is the strength of my life; of whom shall I be afraid?" (Psalms 27:1).

"If the Son therefore shall make you free, ye shall be free indeed" (John 8:36).

The Curse: Palsy and Strokes

The Blessing:

"Thy vows are upon me, O God: I will render praises unto thee. For thou hast delivered my soul from death: wilt not thou deliver my feet from falling, that I may walk before God in the light of the living?" (Psalms 56:12,13).

The Curse: Poisoning

The Blessing:

"They shall take up serpents; and if they drink any deadly thing, it shall not hurt them; . . . " (Mark 16:18).

"Thou hast clothed me with skin and flesh, and hast fenced me with bones and sinews. Thou hast granted me life and favour, and thy visitation hath preserved my spirit" (Job 10:11).

The Curse: Poverty

The Blessing:

"But my God shall supply all your need according to his riches in glory by Christ Jesus" (Philippians 4:19).

"This book of the law shall not depart out of thy mouth; but thou shalt meditate therein day and night, that thou mayest observe to do according to all that is written therein: for then thou shalt make thy way prosperous, and then thou shalt have good success" (Joshua 1:8).

"Blessed is the man that walketh not in the counsel of the ungodly, nor standeth in the way of sinners, nor sitteth in the seat of the scornful. But his delight is in the law of the LORD; and in his law doth he meditate day and night. And he shall be like a tree planted by the rivers of water, that bringeth forth his fruit in his season; his leaf also shall not wither; and whatsoever he doeth shall prosper" (Psalms 1:1-3).

"But seek ye first the kingdom of God, and his righteousness; and all these things shall be added unto you" (Matthew 6:33).

"But thou shalt remember the LORD thy God: for it is he that giveth thee power to get wealth, . . . " (Deuteronomy 8:18).

"Beloved, I wish above all things that thou mayest prosper and be in health, even as thy soul prospereth" (III John 2).

"The thief cometh not, but for to steal, and to kill, and to destroy: I am come that they might have life, and that they might have it more abundantly" (John 10:10).

"Honour the LORD with thy substance, and with the firstfruits of all thine increase: So shall thy barns be filled with plenty, and thy presses shall burst out with new wine" (Proverbs 3:9,10).

"Give, and it shall be given unto you; good measure, pressed down, and shaken together, and running over, shall men give into your bosom. For with the same measure that ye mete withal

it shall be measured to you again" (Luke 6:38).

"Beloved, if our heart condemn us not, then have we confidence toward God. And whatsoever we ask, we receive of him, because we keep his commandments, and do those things that are pleasing in his sight" (I John 3:21,22).

The Curse: Profanity

The Blessing:

"But now ye also put off all these; anger, wrath, malice, blasphemy, filthy communication out of your mouth" (Colossians 3:8).

"Pleasant words are as an honeycomb, sweet to the soul, and health to the bones" (Proverbs 16:24).

"Death and life are in the power of the tongue: and they that love it shall eat the fruit thereof" (Proverbs 18:21).

"A wholesome tongue is a tree of life: . . . " (Proverbs 15:4).

The Curse: Rebellious Children

The Blessing:

"My son, attend to my words; incline thine ear unto my sayings. Let them not depart from thine eyes; keep them in the midst of thine heart. For they are life unto those that find them, and health to all their flesh" (Proverbs 4:20-22).

"Thus saith the LORD; Refrain thy voice from weeping, and thine eyes from tears: for thy work shall be rewarded, saith

the LORD; and they shall come again from the land of the enemy" (Jeremiah 31:16).

The Curse: Sadness and Sorrow

The Blessing:

"Thou wilt shew me the path of life: in thy presence is fulness of joy; at thy right hand there are pleasures for evermore" (Psalms 16:11).

"Then he said unto them, Go your way, eat the fat, and drink the sweet, and send portions unto them for whom nothing is prepared: for this day is holy unto our Lord: neither be ye sorry; for the joy of the LORD is your strength" (Nehemiah 8:10).

"And ye now therefore have sorrow: but I will see you again, and your heart shall rejoice, and your joy no man taketh from you" (John 16:22).

"Whom having not seen, ye love; in whom, though now ye see him not, yet believing, ye rejoice with joy unspeakable and full of glory" (I Peter 1:8).

"But none of these things move me, neither count I my life dear unto myself, so that I might finish my course with joy, . . . " (Acts 20:24).

The Curse: Selfishness and Greed

The Blessing:

"For God so loved the world, that he gave his only begotten Son, that whosoever believeth in him should not perish, but *have everlasting life"* (John 3:16).

"... It is more blessed to give than to receive" (Acts 20:35).

"Will a man rob God? Yet ye have robbed me. But ye say, Wherein have we robbed thee? In tithes and offerings. Ye are cursed with a curse: for ye have robbed me, even this whole nation. Bring ye all the tithes into the storehouse, that there may be meat in mine house, and prove me now herewith, saith the LORD of hosts, if I will not open you the windows of heaven, and pour you out a blessing, that there shall not be room enough to receive it. And I will rebuke the devourer for your sakes, and he shall not destroy the fruits of your ground; neither shall your vine cast her fruit before the time in the field, saith the LORD of hosts. And all nations shall call you blessed: for ye shall be a delightsome land, saith the LORD of hosts" (Malachi 3:8-12).

"There is that scattereth, and yet increaseth; and there is that withholdeth more than is meet, but it tendeth to poverty" (Proverbs 11:24).

"But this I say, He which soweth sparingly shall reap also sparingly; and he which soweth bountifully shall reap also bountifully. Every man according as he purposeth in his heart, so let him give; not grudgingly, or of necessity: for God loveth a cheerful giver" (II Corinthians 9:6,7).

The Curse: Self-Consciousness

The Blessing:

"The fear of man bringeth a snare: but whoso putteth his trust in the LORD shall be safe" (Proverbs 29:25).

The Curse: Smoking

The Blessing:

"He hath delivered my soul in peace from the battle that was against me: . . . " (Psalms 55:18).

"For I the LORD *thy God will hold thy right hand, saying unto thee, Fear not; I will help thee"* (Isaiah 41:13).

"Know ye not that ye are the temple of God, and that the Spirit of God dwelleth in you? If any man defile the temple of God, him shall God destroy; for the temple of God is holy, which temple ye are" (I Corinthians 3:16,17).

"Thou shalt come to thy grave in a full age, like as a shock of corn cometh in in his season" (Job 5:26).

" . . . For this purpose the Son of God was manifested, that he might destroy the works of the devil" (I John 3:8).

The Curse: Sorrow

The Blessing:

"This is the day which the LORD *hath made; we will rejoice and be glad in it"* (Psalms 118:24).

"Make a joyful noise unto the LORD, *all ye lands. Serve the* LORD *with gladness: come before his presence with singing. Know ye that the* LORD *he is God: it is he that hath made us, and not we ourselves; we are his people, and the sheep of his pasture. Enter into his gates with thanksgiving, and into his courts with praise: be thankful unto him, and bless his name.*

For the LORD is good; his mercy is everlasting; and his truth endureth to all generations" (Psalms 100:1-5).

"A merry heart maketh a cheerful countenance: but by sorrow of the heart the spirit is broken" (Proverbs 15:13).

"Fear thou not; for I am with thee: be not dismayed; for I am thy God: I will strengthen thee; yea, I will help thee; yea, I will uphold thee with the right hand of my righteousness" (Isaiah 41:10).

The Curse: Ulcers

The Blessing:

"He healeth the broken in heart, and bindeth up their wounds" (Psalms 147:3).

The Curse: Unforgiveness, Bitterness

The Blessing:

"And when ye stand praying, forgive, if ye have ought against any: that your Father also which is in heaven may forgive you your trespasses. But if ye do not forgive, neither will your Father which is in heaven forgive your trespasses" (Mark 11:25,26).

"But I say unto you, Love your enemies, bless them that curse you, do good to them that hate you, and pray for them which despitefully use you, and persecute you; That ye may be the children of your Father which is in heaven: for he maketh his sun to rise on the evil and on the good, and sendeth rain on the just and on the unjust" (Matthew 5:44,45).

The Curse: Unsaved Family

The Blessing:

"And they said, Believe on the Lord Jesus Christ, and thou shalt be saved, and thy house" (Acts 16:31).

"Then Peter said unto them, Repent, and be baptized every one of you in the name of Jesus Christ for the remission of sins, and ye shall receive the gift of the Holy Ghost. For the promise is unto you, and to your children, and to all that are afar off, even as many as the Lord our God shall call" (Acts 2:38,39).

" . . . rejoice, because your names are written in heaven" (Luke 10:20).

"For whosoever shall call upon the name of the Lord shall be saved" (Romans 10:13).

The Curse: Unsaved Loved Ones

The Blessing:

"That if thou shalt confess with thy mouth the Lord Jesus, and shalt believe in thine heart that God hath raised him from the dead, thou shalt be saved. For with the heart man believeth unto righteousness; and with the mouth confession is made unto salvation" (Romans 10:9,10).

The Curse: Untimely Death

The Blessing:

"Ye shall walk in all the ways which the LORD your God hath

commanded you, that ye may live, and that it may be well with you, and that ye may prolong your days in the land which ye shall possess" (Deuteronomy 5:33).

The Curse: Unworthiness

The Blessing:

"For he hath made him to be sin for us, who knew no sin; that we might be made the righteousness of God in him" (II Corinthians 5:21).

The Curse: Wounds

The Blessing:

"For I will restore health unto thee, and I will heal thee of thy wounds, saith the LORD; . . . " (Jeremiah 30:17).

The Curse: Worries, Frustration

The Blessing:

"Delight thyself also in the LORD; and he shall give thee the desires of thine heart" (Psalms 37:4).

"Casting all your care upon him; for he careth for you" (I Peter 5:7).

"Rejoice in the Lord alway: and again I say, Rejoice" (Philippians 4:4).

"Not that I speak in respect of want: for I have learned, in whatsoever state I am, therewith to be content" (Philippians 4:11).

"Be careful for nothing; but in every thing by prayer and supplication with thanksgiving let your requests be made known unto God. And the peace of God, which passeth all understanding, shall keep your hearts and minds through Christ Jesus" (Philippians 4:6,7).

Receive Jesus Christ as Lord and Savior of Your Life.

The Bible says, "That if thou shalt confess with thy mouth the Lord Jesus, and shalt believe in thine heart that God hath raised him from the dead, thou shalt be saved. For with the heart man believeth unto righteousness; and with the mouth confession is made unto salvation" (Romans 10:9,10).

To receive Jesus Christ as Lord and Savior of your life, sincerely pray this prayer from your heart:

Dear Jesus,

I believe that You died for me and that You rose again on the third day. I confess to You that I am a sinner and that I need Your love and forgiveness. Come into my life, forgive my sins, and give me eternal life. I confess You now as my Lord. Thank You for my salvation!

Signed _____

Date _____

Write to us.

We will send you information to help you with your new life in Christ.

Marilyn Hickey Ministries • P.O. Box 17340
Denver, CO 80217 • (303) 770-0400

Prayer Requests

Let us join our faith with yours for your prayer needs. Fill out the coupon below and send to Marilyn Hickey Ministries, P.O. Box 17340, Denver, CO 80217.

Prayer Request _____

_____

_____

_____

_____

_____

Mr. & Mrs.
Mr.   Please print.
Miss
Name Mrs. _____

Address _____

City _____

State _____ Zip _____

Phone (H) (   ) _____

   (W) (   ) _____

☐ If you want prayer immediately, call our Prayer Center at
   (303) 796-1333, Monday – Friday, 4 a.m. – 4:30 p.m. (MT).

For Your Information

Free Monthly Magazine

☐ Please send me your free monthly magazine OUTPOURING (including daily devotionals, timely articles, and ministry updates)!

Tapes and Books

☐ Please send me Marilyn's latest product catalog.

Name ^{Mr. & Mrs.} ^{Miss} ^{Mrs.} ^{Mr.} _____

Please Print

Address_____

City_____

State_____ Zip_____

Phone (H) (___) _____

(W) (___) _____

Mail to
Marilyn Hickey Ministries
P.O. Box 17340
Denver, CO 80217

WORD
to the
WORLD
COLLEGE

Explore your options and increase your knowledge of the Word at this unique college of higher learning for men and women of faith. Word to the World College offers **on-campus and correspondence courses** that give you the opportunity to learn from Marilyn Hickey and other great Bible scholars. WWC can help prepare you to be an effective minister of the gospel. Classes are open to both full- and part-time students.

For more information, complete the coupon below and send it to:

- -

**Word to the World College
P.O. Box 17340
Denver, CO 80217
(303) 770-0400**

Mr.   Please print.
Mrs.
Name Miss _____

Address_____

City _____ State _____ Zip _____

Phone (H) _____ (W) _____

BOOKS BY MARILYN HICKEY

A Cry for Miracles ($7.95)
Acts of the Holy Spirit ($7.95)
Angels All Around ($7.95)
Armageddon ($4.95)
Ask Marilyn ($9.95)
Be Healed ($9.95)
Blessing Journal ($4.95)
Bible Encounter Classic
  Edition ($24.95)
Book of Revelation Comic
  Book (The) ($3.00)
Break the Generation Curse
  ($7.95)
Break the Generation Curse
  Part 2 ($9.95)
Daily Devotional ($7.95)
Dear Marilyn ($7.95)
Devils, Demons, and
  Deliverance ($9.95)
Divorce Is Not the Answer
  ($7.95)
Especially for Today's
  Woman ($14.95)
Freedom From Bondages
  ($7.95)
Gift-Wrapped Fruit ($2.95)

God's Covenant for Your Family
  ($7.95)
God's Rx for a Hurting Heart ($4.95)
Hebrew Honey ($14.95)
How to Be a Mature Christian ($7.95)
Know Your Ministry ($4.95)
Maximize Your Day…God's Way
  ($7.95)
Names of God (The) ($7.95)
Nehemiah—Rebuilding the Broken
  Places in Your Life ($7.95)
No. 1 Key to Success—Meditation
  (The) ($4.95)
Proverbs Classic Library Edition
  ($24.95)
Release the Power of the Blood
  Covenant ($4.95)
Satan-Proof Your Home ($7.95)
Save the Family Promise Book
  ($14.95)
Signs in the Heavens ($7.95)
What Every Person Wants to Know
  About Prayer ($4.95)
When Only a Miracle Will Do ($4.95)
Your Miracle Source ($4.95)
Your Total Health Handbook—
  Body • Soul • Spirit ($9.95)

MINI-BOOKS: $1.00 each
by Marilyn Hickey

Beat Tension
Bold Men Win
Bulldog Faith
Change Your Life
Children Who Hit the Mark
Conquering Setbacks
Don't Park Here
Experience Long Life
Fasting and Prayer
God's Benefit: Healing
God's Seven Keys to Make
  You Rich
Hold On to Your Dream
How to Become More Than
  a Conqueror
How to Win Friends

I Can Be Born Again and Spirit Filled
I Can Dare to Be an Achiever
Keys to Healing Rejection
Power of Forgiveness (The)
Power of the Blood (The)
Receiving Resurrection Power
Renew Your Mind
Solving Life's Problems
Speak the Word
Standing in the Gap
Story of Esther (The)
Tithes • Offerings • Alms •
  God's Plan for Blessing You
Turning Point
Winning Over Weight
Women of the Word

Prices are in U.S. dollars. If ordering in foreign currency, calculate the current exchange rate

Marilyn Hickey Ministries

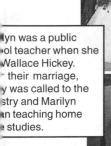

yn was a public
ol teacher when she
Wallace Hickey.
their marriage,
y was called to the
stry and Marilyn
n teaching home
studies.

he vision of Marilyn Hickey Ministries
"cover the earth with the Word"
iah 11:9). For over 30 years Marilyn
key has dedicated herself to an
nted, unique, and distinguished ministry
aching out to people—from all walks of
—who are hungry for God's Word and all
He has for them. Millions have
essed and acclaimed the positive,
sonal impact she brings through fresh
elation knowledge that God has given
through His Word.

Marilyn has been the invited guest of
ernment leaders and heads of state
many nations of the world. She is
sidered by many to be one of today's
atest ambassadors of God's Good News
his dark and hurting generation.

he more Marilyn follows God's will for
life, the more God uses her to bring
eshing, renewal, and revival to the Body
hrist throughout the world. As His
dient servant, Marilyn desires to follow
all the days of her life.

Marilyn and Wally adopted
their son Michael; through a
fulfilled prophecy they had
their daughter Sarah, who with
her husband Reece, is now
part of the ministry.

Marilyn founded her ministry "Life for Laymen" so that she could reach more people with her gift for practical Bible application.

Marilyn taught at Denver's "Happy Church" and hosted ministry conferences with husband Wally.

At a retreat in 1976, Marilyn realized she was called to "cover the earth with the Word."

The ministry staff in the early days helped Marilyn answer the mail that came in response to her first 15-minute radio show.

Soon Marilyn realized how many more people she could reach by going on television. She and Wally hosted many well known guests.

In Guatemala with former President Ephraim Rios-Mott

Marilyn has been the invited guest of government leaders and heads of state from many nations of the world.

In Egypt with Mrs. Anwar Sadat

In Venezuela with first lady Mrs. Perez

In Lebanon with Major Haddad

Marilyn ministers to guerillas in Honduras and brings food and clothing to the wives and children who are encamped with their husbands.

The popular Bible reading plan "Time With Him" began in 1978 and invited people to "read through the Bible with Marilyn." The monthly ministry magazine has since been renamed "Outpouring." It now includes a calendar of ministry events, timely articles, and featured product offers.

Through Word to the World College (formerly Marilyn [Hic]key Bible College), Marilyn [is h]elping to equip men and [wo]men to take the gospel [aro]und the world.

[Re]cently dorms [we]re added to the [ca]mpus facilities.

National Women's Conferences and Pastor's Wives' Conventions were held across the U.S., exhorting women to "Change Their World!"

God began to open doors for the supplying of Bibles to many foreign lands—China, Israel, Poland, Ethiopia, Russia, Romania, and Ukraine, just to name a few.

The only woman on the board of directors of Dr. Cho's church in Korea, Marilyn has spoken at his church many times and has also been a featured speaker at the Church Growth Conference held in Japan.

An international satellite broadcast was simulcast live from Israel to U.S. cities.

As famine and war ravaged many African countries, Marilyn began a series of trips to refugee camps, supplying food for feeding programs and Bibles for the largely communist communities.

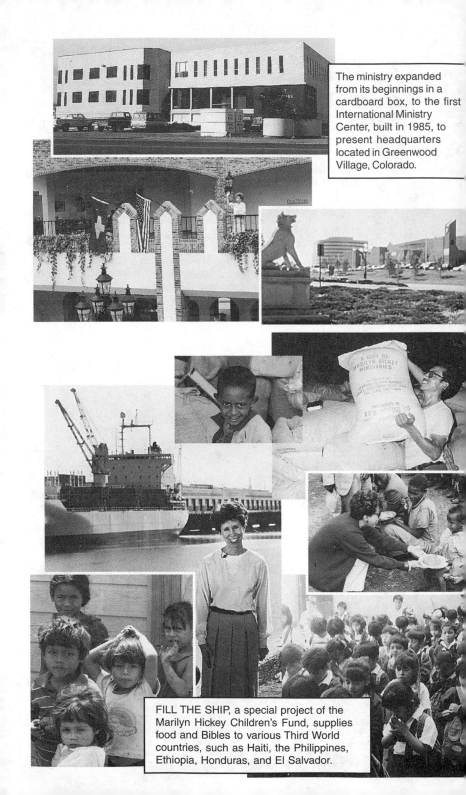

The ministry expanded from its beginnings in a cardboard box, to the first International Ministry Center, built in 1985, to present headquarters located in Greenwood Village, Colorado.

FILL THE SHIP, a special project of the Marilyn Hickey Children's Fund, supplies food and Bibles to various Third World countries, such as Haiti, the Philippines, Ethiopia, Honduras, and El Salvador.

The prime time television special, "A Cry for Miracles," featured co-host Gavin MacLeod.

Over 1,500 ministry products help people in all areas of their life.

Marilyn Hickey's Prayer Center handles calls from all over the U.S.—ministering to those who need agreement in prayer.

Marilyn ministered in underground churches in Romania before any of the European communist countries were officially open.

Ministry and speaking engagement at a Women's Conference in Nigeria

Marilyn receives her honorary doctorate from Oral Roberts University

Marilyn and her Faith Covenant Partners respond to countless needs across the world ... the devastating earthquakes in Mexico City, Romanian orphans, leprosy victims in Africa, orphans in war torn Rwanda, street children in Brazil, ... all are touched by God's power.

lyn has been a guest
eral times on the 700 Club
host Pat Robertson.

Airlift Manila provided much needed food,
Bibles, and personal supplies to the
Philippines; MHM also raised funds to aid in
the digging of water wells for those without
clean drinking water.

Marilyn participates in a "devil-stomp" on prayer requests: thousands are received daily from friends and partners all over the world and are prayed over by Marilyn and the staff.

MHM supports Mission of Mercy in Calcutta, headed by Huldah Buntain. Marilyn has made several trips there.

Missions' trips to China are really close to Marilyn's and Sarah's hearts. Thousands of Bibles have been smuggled across the borde

"Today With Marilyn" Bible teaching program is broadcast weekdays on TBN, BET, and several independent stations. The program is also seen overseas by millions through Christian Network TV, in Australia on Network 10, and in more than 80 other countries worldwide.

Marilyn ministers to and teaches thousands at Encounters and Miracle Healing Crusades overseas, as well as in the U.S.

Exciting ministry opportunities awaited Marilyn and her team of travelers in Ukraine and Russia, as the doors opened for the Gospel.

Victim of the nuclear power plant disaster in Chernobyl

Marilyn has held Bible Encounters in Malaysia and Singapore. While traveling through Hong Kong she ministered to Vietnamese in a refugee camp.

Ministry trips and cruises to places such as Indonesia, Russia, Greece, Ukraine, Turkey, and Israel offer short-term missions' opportunities to travel with Marilyn to exotic places.

Overseas offices have recently been set up in the United Kingdom, Australia, and South Africa. Marilyn also hosts yearly meetings, crusades, and missions' projects in those countries.

Crowds of up to 200,000 attended the open-air crusade in Bangalore, India.

In Islamabad, Pakistan, Marilyn held Ministry Training Schools. Total crusade attendance was estimated at 70,000.

Eritrea and Sudan—Ministry Training Schools, nightly crusades and Madagascar crusade with Sarah and Marilyn ministering